The FRIENDSHIP BOOK

of Francis Gay

D. C. THOMSON & CO., LTD.
London Glasgow Manchester Dundee

A Thought For Each Day In 1981

" I count myself in nothing else so happy, as in a soul remembering my good friends."

From Richard II by William Shakespeare.

JANUARY

THURSDAY—JANUARY 1.

LORD, grant me I pray
Courage when the best things fail me,
Calm and poise when storms assail me,
Commonsense when things perplex me,
Sense of humour when they vex me,
Hope when disappointments damp me,
Wider vision when life cramps me,
Kindness when folk need it badly,
Readiness to help them gladly,
And when effort seems in vain
Wisdom to begin again.

FRIDAY—JANUARY 2.

TODAY I found a feather tucked between the pages of a book. It reminded me of an old lady I knew. She was housebound and one of her greatest pleasures was to watch the birds splashing in a birdbath outside her window. One day she asked me to refill the bath, so out I went. Lying beside it I found this lovely yellowish-green feather, which she told me a greenfinch had shed.

As I fingered this boyhood treasure it occurred to me that we are all like that greenfinch. Day by day we each leave part of ourselves behind. Those are the parts that tell others what kind of people we really are. What do I leave? Kindly words and helpful deeds, or cross words and unkind actions?

Perhaps the start of a new year is a good time to resolve to be more careful of the imprint that we leave on each passing day. A year helpfully lived will surely leave few regrets.

SATURDAY—JANUARY 3.

CRISP snow crunched under my feet in spite of the brilliant sunshine. I shivered in the cold wind, turned up my coat collar and plodded on, head down.

"Hello, Mr Gay. Great to be out, isn't it?" said a cheery voice.

I looked up to meet the smiling eyes of Jim, a crippled teenager who attends our local church. In spite of his lameness, he was obviously enjoying his walk in the snow and his face glowed with happiness and contentment.

"Good to be alive on a day like this," he beamed as he limped past, and suddenly I felt ashamed. The road was a carpet of sparkling virgin snow, but I had scarcely noticed. A vast blue canopy was spread above me, but I had not looked up to admire it.

I threw back my shoulders, took a deep breath and walked on at a smarter pace—grateful to young Jim whose friendly greeting had helped to make it a truly glorious day for me, too.

SUNDAY—JANUARY 4.

THE Lord bless thee, and keep thee. The Lord make his face to shine upon thee, and be gracious unto thee.

MONDAY—JANUARY 5.

IF you can lend a needed hand,
Or someone's sorrow share,
If you can show by word or deed
You sympathise and care,
Please do it now—for if you wait
Another day could be too late.

TUESDAY—JANUARY 6.

A CLERGYMAN and one of his elderly parishioners were walking home from church one frosty day when the old gentleman slipped and fell flat on his back. The minister looked at him for a moment, and then, assured that he was not really hurt, commented wryly, " Friend, sinners stand on slippery places."

The old gentleman looked up as if to reassure himself of the fact, and then said, " I see they do—but I can't!"

WEDNESDAY—JANUARY 7.

AT a recent family gathering Katie, a young niece whom I seldom see, climbed on to my lap. Almost immediately my other niece, Joanna, who was then about three, tried to join her. I moved Katie to one knee so that Joanna could climb on to the other. With a scowl, Katie leaned forward to push her rival away but Joanna completely disarmed her by kissing her on the cheek! Katie's astonished look changed to a smile and both little girls shared my lap happily.

On our return home, the Lady of the House and I smiled at the new neighbour who had recently moved in opposite. She glared, slammed the gate she had come out to shut, and marched indoors.

" It won't be easy to make friends there," I sighed.

" Just wait," she said. " A little love goes a long way."

I must confess that (not for the first time!) her wisdom filled me with admiration. For, do you know, I hadn't got round to telling her about Katie and Joanna then!

THURSDAY—JANUARY 8.

I HAD struggled through the driving snow with a small parcel of groceries which the Lady of the House had asked me to bring. Now I was standing at the window, drinking steaming coffee and telling her of the horrible conditions I had just conquered. She suddenly interrupted me.

"There's poor Andrew looking out. He must be terribly fed-up with this weather."

I hadn't thought of it—but how right she was. Andrew is not seriously ill but he has a heart condition that makes walking in strong winds and severe cold very dangerous.

We'd been having weeks of this kind of weather and all that time Andrew, a very good neighbour of ours, had never been out.

So what was I to do but feel thoroughly ashamed for not having thought before about what the Lady of the House had said, put on my coat and go and knock on Andrew's door.

Andrew was so pleased to have a visitor. I didn't stay long, but I promised to go again soon. And back home I thought of how many people there are like Andrew and how very easily we can brighten their day.

FRIDAY—JANUARY 9.

YOUNG Mums can get very, very tired. But when they least expect it, suddenly they will receive a reward that makes all their hard work worthwhile. Mrs Oakley wrote to tell me of one such reward. She said that at the end of a rather trying day she was tucking up Jimmy for the night when she realised he was staring at her. Then suddenly he said, "I don't know who taught you to be a mummy, but they did a really good job!"

MIRACLE

" Only God can make a tree "
—We know the song is right,
And only He can change its face
Silently, overnight.

SATURDAY—JANUARY 10.

WHEN good friends walk beside us,
On the trails that we must keep,
Our burdens seem less heavy,
And the hills are not so steep,
The weary miles pass swiftly,
Taken in a joyous stride,
And all the world seems brighter,
When friends walk by our side.

SUNDAY—JANUARY 11.

AND God said, Let there be light: and there was light.

MONDAY—JANUARY 12.

I THINK that one of the nicest things that can happen is to have your name given to a beautiful plant. I was admiring some heather plants in a bit of garden Mrs Jackson had just " broken in " and pointed to one I specially liked, a beautiful soft pink.

" Oh, that's a Cornish heath," said Mrs Jackson. " It's called ' Mrs D.F. Maxwell '."

" It's a beauty," I said. " But why the name?"

" I can answer that," she said. " Mr and Mrs Maxwell were on honeymoon in Cornwall fifty years ago. They were gathering mushrooms when they saw this unusual colour. They knew they had found something quite new so they cut a few young shoots, wrapped them in moss and brought them home."

I bought one of the heaths and now, every time I look at it in my garden I remember that I owe its beauty to a young couple who were enjoying a honeymoon in Cornwall half a century ago.

TUESDAY—JANUARY 13.

A HAMPSHIRE man of 89 was asked his recipe for a long, healthy, and happy life.

He replied, "My formula lies in two simple words: 'Yes, dear!'"

WEDNESDAY—JANUARY 14.

I CONFESS that, like most people, there are times when I retaliate rather crossly when something irritates me—especially if I am interrupted in the middle of something important. So I was quite heartened to find an instance of a famous saint showing a bit of normal irritability. It is said that the great 11th century Saint Bernard was in the middle of preparing a sermon when he was interrupted by flies swarming round him, buzzing loudly. The saint was so annoyed that he paused in his preaching—and excommunicated them!

THURSDAY—JANUARY 15.

I AM grateful to Leslie Norman of Rochester, Kent, for sending me these maxims from his scrapbook:

It is important that people know what they stand for. It is equally important that they know what they won't stand for.

It is better to see crosswords printed in the daily paper than to hear cross words spoken daily in the home.

Evil owes much of its success not to the strength of its supporters but to the inaction of its opponents.

The mind is like a parachute—no use unless it is open.

CERTAINTIES

As sure's the night must follow day,
As sure's no dawn can ever stay,
As sure as clouds across the sky
Will always and forever fly,
So surely, too, will small birds sing
And flowers bloom when breaks the Spring.

FRIDAY—JANUARY 16.

IT is not only great men and women who change the world. We all can in our own small way. Our little part of the world will become different because of us and will be changed for the better if we lead the sort of lives we should. The poet Longfellow put this thought into these words:

Lives of great men all remind us
We can make our lives sublime,
And, departing, leave behind us
Footprints on the sands of time.

SATURDAY—JANUARY 17.

I HAPPENED to meet John Gray as we were walking to church. It was a bitter day, and I complimented him on the very smart hat he was wearing—one of those furry-looking pieces of headware you see in all the pictures which show Russia in wintertime.

"I have two of them," he smiled. "My wife gave me one a couple of Christmasses ago. And my daughter, who didn't know I had one, gave me one last Christmas."

"So you're well equipped," I said. "Well, I only hope the winter is going to last long enough for you to need *two* Russian hats."

A sudden gust of wind made us both huddle into our overcoats. I said something uncomplimentary about the weather.

"But it's much better than last year," said John.

I didn't think it was, but before I could say anything he added: "I was in hospital for three months last winter. So it's bound to be better, isn't it?"

Of course!

SUNDAY—JANUARY 18.

FREELY ye have received, freely give.

MONDAY—JANUARY 19.

SOME time ago there was a television programme about the Whitechapel Bell Foundry in London. It has been making bells and sending them all over the world for over 400 years. Big Ben was made there too. We saw men busy fashioning hand-bells, and some testing them for the right pitch. The family of one of the craftsmen had been connected with the Foundry for over 250 years.

It was not until that evening that I learned that Britain is known as "The Ringing Isle." I understand that there are fifty thousand bell-ringers ringing about eighty thousand bells!

I recently heard some Whitechapel hand-bells. They belonged to the Southminster Hand-bell ringers of Pittsburg, Pennsylvania, USA and they were playing hymn tunes on them here in Britain to the glory of God. They had rung their way around the world from Whitechapel and back again.

This great missionary effort, which started in Whitechapel all those years ago, is still spreading today, with the help and care of British craftsmen.

TUESDAY—JANUARY 20.

A MAN I know recently visited the town's smart new dentist's surgery. As he got anxiously into the dentist's chair he said, "I'm sorry to be so nervous, this is my first filling."

"Oh, don't worry," said the dentist, "It's mine, too!"

WEDNESDAY—JANUARY 21.

WHEN my friend Sandy became Governor of a Rotary district for a year, it meant he and his wife had to change their entire way of life. For a whole year they had to visit and speak at Rotary Clubs all over the country and abroad. They had to attend luncheons, dinners, dances, prize-givings and anniversaries and to accept the hospitality of people they scarcely knew.

After his term of office was over I asked Sandy if there was anything he had found particularly difficult. He thought for a long time before he answered: " We found goodwill everywhere," he said. " But right at the beginning I realised that for a whole year my opinions had to take second place to those of the folk I was meeting."

I can think of few things more difficult, but I can tell you that Sandy earned great praise during his year of office. And after hearing that remark of his I think I knew exactly why.

THURSDAY—JANUARY 22.

JANUARY 22nd, 1979, is a day to remember for a Lancashire housewife. That was the day her dream was realised. The campaign she had initiated to raise one and a half million pounds for a " magic eye " scanner had reached its target, and she laid the foundation stone of the wing which will house the machine at Manchester's Christie Hospital. The equipment can detect cancer at a very early stage and so could save the lives of many sufferers.

And what does the campaigner think of it all? " I have no intention of leaving this life for a long time yet. I'm far too busy."

Well spoken, Pat Seed, M.B.E.

IN HARMONY

Whatever it is that needs to be done,
Doing it together makes it fun!

FRIDAY—JANUARY 23.

A NUMBER of years ago a journalist interviewed Mrs C. H. Haldane, wife of a well-known Wakefield historian, in their historic home Clarke Hall (now a fine and unusual school museum). At the end of the interview elderly Mrs Haldane gave the following excellent recipe for happiness:

"To equal quantities of generosity and thought for others, add a few drops of pleasant smiles, followed by the same number of kind words. Sprinkle freely with fun and merriment, flavour with wit and humour, and mix thoroughly with the spirit of love; warm with bright looks and serve immediately. Specially desired at Christmas, but seasonal at any time."

SATURDAY—JANUARY 24.

FIVE-YEAR-OLD Malcolm was a lovable, talkative little boy. He seemed to have boundless energy from morning till night, and there were times when he almost exhausted his devoted parents. One afternoon a kindly Scots minister—a friend of the family—called at the house. After a short while he brought Malcolm into the general conversation.

"Tell me, do you say your prayers every night?"

Malcolm stared at the carpet. "Not every night."

"Indeed! And how is that?" asked the minister, his eyes twinkling.

The boy looked up and smiled. "Daddy says them for me. When he carries me upstairs he often says—"Well, thank God you'll soon be fast asleep and the house will be quiet."

Malcolm paused, "And then I say 'Amen'."

SUNDAY—JANUARY 25.

TAKE therefore no thought for the morrow: for the morrow shall take thought for the things of itself.

MONDAY—JANUARY 26.

I HAD a friendly smile—
I gave that smile away;
The milkman and the postman
Seemed glad of it each day.

I took it out when shopping;
I had it in the street;
I gave it—without thinking—
To all I chanced to meet.

I gave the little ones my smile;
And though I'd much to do,
I gave it to my neighbours—
The old folks had it, too.

I always give my smile away
As thoughtless as can be;
Yet every time—how wonderful—
My smile returns to me!

TUESDAY—JANUARY 27.

A READER in Hereford made me smile with this story. Apparently a woman was telling the wife of a vicar that she firmly believed that there was always a place in heaven for the wives of clergymen.

The vicar's wife thought for a moment and then said, " Oh, but I'd much rather stay with my husband!"

WEDNESDAY—JANUARY 28.

GRANDFATHERS are wonderful, aren't they? A lady I know was telling me how well she remembered her grandfather coming to stay when she was a small girl. "He always had a secret to share with me and I can still feel his beard tickle my cheek as he stooped to whisper it in my ear."

Grandpa's secrets came in two categories: Sound Advice and Important Truth. "If I could tell him which kind of secret it was, he would reward me with one of those big pre-decimal pennies!"

She still remembered some of the secrets, too, particularly this one: "The heart is never emptied by loving, nor the purse emptied by giving."

Sound Advice? Yes, and an Important Truth, too, I would say.

THURSDAY—JANUARY 29.

I WAS watching some dogs being trained to compete in the Obedience Championships at the world-famous Crufts Dog-show. The instructor put the owners and their dogs through the usual paces with familiar commands like "Stay!", "Seek!" and so forth.

Then she gave the most important instruction of all: "Now, praise your dogs!" And it was a delight to see how the dogs responded to a few kind words and a stroke or a pat—just a simple acknowledgment to show that they had done well. As I watched these dogs wagging their tails I couldn't help thinking that human beings are not so different. Often all we need to keep us going is just a word of encouragement, a pat on the shoulder. Don't you agree?

FRIDAY—JANUARY 30.

EDMUND BURKE, the prominent eighteenth century statesman, possessed a great gift of oratory. After one particularly brilliant and momentous speech, his brother Richard appeared deep in thought.

"I have been wondering how it has come about that Edmund has contrived to monopolise all the talents of our family," he said pensively. "But then again, I remember that when *we* were at play, *he* was always at work!"

A timeless reminder that nothing worthwhile is ever achieved without dedication and sustained effort.

SATURDAY—JANUARY 31.

SOME of the most important archaeological finds are made not with a spade but by looking at aerial photographs. Viewed from a height we can see the outlines of the fields, roads, tracks and ponds of earlier ages. It's an interesting thought that if you have ever dug just a simple trench then you have left a permanent mark on the landscape. A ditch can be traced thousands of years after it has been filled in because the crops grow taller and greener there. We cannot notice things like this on the ground simply because we are too close to them.

Isn't this true also of our lives? We are often able to understand our problems better if we can look at them from a distance. Distance gives a sense of proportion because it highlights what affects the whole rather than the parts. By taking an "aerial view" we can often avoid making a mistake, perhaps through taking ourselves too seriously.

FEBRUARY

SUNDAY—FEBRUARY 1.

LEAD us not into temptation, but deliver us from evil.

MONDAY—FEBRUARY 2.

DO you sometimes waste energy fretting about the future? My friend Christine became so burdened through carrying tomorrow's load on top of the day's cares that she collapsed under the strain.

The doctor advised rest and change so she went to stay with her Aunt Matilda in the country. It was spring and Nature's sweet music soon worked a miracle on her troubled spirit.

In no time she felt calmed and refreshed, and Aunt Matilda put the finishing touch to the cure. On the day Christine left, her aunt took her aside and said, "Now, Christine, remember to live just one day at a time." And then she recited this verse:

Build a little fence of trust
Around today;
Fill the space with loving work,
And therein stay;
Look not through the sheltering bars
Upon tomorrow,
God will help you bear what comes,
Of joy or sorrow.

Christine has never been ill again and I happen to know that she often repeats that verse to herself. Could that have something to do with her good health, do you think? Aunt Matilda would say so!

TUESDAY—FEBRUARY 3.

MY friend George was telling Jenny the story of The Three Bears, while Grandma sat by the fire knitting. Occasionally she would glance over her needles to smile at Jenny whose face was a picture in the firelight as she listened with rapt attention.

When the story was finished, Grandma said quietly, " that's a lovely story, but there are more than three bears, you know."

George and Jenny looked at each other, and then Jenny counted on her fingers. "There's Daddy Bear, there's Mummy Bear and there's Baby Bear—oh, do you mean Teddy Bear?"

Grandma shook her head. "You've missed out the two most important bears of all—*Bear* and *Forbear.*"

George doubts if Jenny completely understood what Grandma meant. But he does, and one day he hopes his daughter will too.

WEDNESDAY—FEBRUARY 4.

WHENEVER I see the February snowdrops I call to mind the legend which says that when Adam and Eve had been sent from the Garden of Eden they entered the world of winter. Adam tried in vain to re-enter the Garden to bring out something of beauty to comfort Eve, but the entrance was guarded by an angel. At last the angel, seeing Eve's distress, took pity. Putting out his hand he caught a snowflake and breathed gently on it. The snowflake blossomed into a flower.

So every snowflake is a promise that in Spring and Summer, flowers will come again to beautify the world.

THURSDAY—FEBRUARY 5.

DYLAN THOMAS, the famous Welsh poet, was certainly a most unusual character. Since his death in 1953 many books and radio scripts have been written about his odd wandering life, but Dylan, as one who knew him well has declared, was not altogether as black as he has been painted. The following story of this gifted, unfortunate man deserves to be more widely known.

One afternoon in his native Swansea, Dylan was walking along the main street when he noticed an old lady weeping quietly outside a florist's shop. Genuinely concerned, Dylan asked her what was wrong. The lady explained that she had come into town that day to buy some flowers to place on her late husband's grave, but she had lost her handbag. Dylan thought hard. He was down to his last two pounds. Then suddenly he dashed into the shop and a few minutes later came out carrying a bunch of red roses which he handed to the old lady.

This erratic genius, whatever his faults, never lacked human compassion.

FRIDAY—FEBRUARY 6.

THE preacher held up a large white handkerchief for his congregation to see. Near the middle of the handkerchief was a small black spot.

"What can you see?" he asked.

"A black spot," someone replied.

"That's strange," said the preacher. "Can't you see a large white handkerchief?"

It is too often like that when we look at each other.

HELLO!

Travelling in comfort is my cup of tea,
In a snug little corner that's sheer luxury!
While lesser breeds envy the transport I use,
I spend all my time in admiring the views!

SATURDAY—FEBRUARY 7.

USUALLY I enjoy Saturdays but not this particular one. I awoke with a headache, dropped our favourite teapot and, later, my latch-key snapped off in the lock. It was one of those days!

Then, in the evening, the Lady of the House called me over to the window. She didn't say anything, but just stood and gazed at the glorious sunset. What a sight it was, the reds and golds blazoned across the sky. Do you wonder I suddenly felt ashamed? I realised I had been letting my own petty trials and cares blind me to the beauties and delights all around me. As I resolved not to allow it to happen again, I wondered if some similar realisation had inspired the poet and hymn-writer John Keble when he penned these lines:

One finger's-breadth at hand will mar
A world of light in heaven afar,
A mote eclipse a glorious star,
An eyelid hide the sky.

SUNDAY—FEBRUARY 8.

THEREFORE all things whatsoever ye would that men should do to you, do ye even so to them.

MONDAY—FEBRUARY 9.

AFTER losing his seat at an election a Member of Parliament was asked if he was disappointed.

"Well, yes, but not too much," he replied. "You see it's nice to be important, but *much more important to be nice.*"

TUESDAY—FEBRUARY 10.

IT'S wonderful when someone needs
From you a helping hand,
And thanks you with a grateful heart
Because you understand.
It's wonderful when folk are glad
Because they know you're near,
That in their world, because of you,
A star of hope shines clear.

WEDNESDAY—FEBRUARY 11.

AS every writer knows, one of the most important things in his craft is making a good start. Probably few of us today read that old favourite "The Cloister and the Hearth." But its author, Charles Reade, begins it with one of the most inspiring thoughts possible:

"Not a day passes over the earth, but men and women of no note do great deeds, speak great words and suffer noble sorrows."

THURSDAY—FEBRUARY 12.

SO often we hear it said: "But he (or she) had all the luck."

Well, there's no doubt that some people seem to have more than their share of good fortune, but I often think of a comment of Gary Player, the South African golfer.

After one of his many successes someone said to him, "But don't you think you were pretty lucky that you had so little trouble getting out of bunkers!"

Player nodded his head in agreement. Then he added: "But I find, too, that the more I practise *the luckier I seem to get.*"

FRIDAY—FEBRUARY 13.

ON her first attendance at Sunday school, four-year-old Wendy heard the chorus which begins:

God is still on the throne
And he will remember His own . . .

Next day the little girl's mother heard Wendy singing the same words over and over again—but she hadn't got them quite right. Wendy was singing: " God is still on the phone."

In a way Wendy had a point, hadn't she? Perhaps some of us would pray more often if we remembered that God is always there and far more ready to listen than we are to speak to Him.

SATURDAY—FEBRUARY 14.

HAVE you received a Valentine card today? Or thought of sending one? I must confess that I like traditions of this kind, and St. Valentine's Day is one of the most delightful of our ancient customs.

Since St. Valentine was said to have died on the 14th February, on the eve of the Roman festival of Lupercalia, some of the customs of that day have been associated with the name Valentine.

An old idea, mentioned by Chaucer, is that birds choose their mates on Valentine's Day. And, of course, for many centuries it has been the custom for humans to send an anonymous message of love producing plenty of serious expectation—and harmless fun.

I think it's a splendid idea to let someone know that you love them—and it's not just for young sweethearts, either. Long live Valentine's Day!

SUNDAY—FEBRUARY 15.

WHOSOEVER will be chief among you, let him be your servant.

MONDAY—FEBRUARY 16.

I WONDER if I am wrong in thinking that the happiest folk are those who think least about money. Even some millionaires might agree with me!

That very wealthy American, John D. Rockefeller, once told a Bible Class that he believed it was every man's duty to get all the money he could fairly and honestly and to give away all he could.

"What is success?" he asked. "Is it money? Some of you have all the money you need to provide your wants. The poorest man in the world is the man who has *nothing but money.*"

TUESDAY—FEBRUARY 17.

THE well-known television personality, Cyril Fletcher, once told viewers the secret of his long and successful marriage. Admitting that he was very romantic, he described how every wedding anniversary he takes his wife into the famous church of St. Martin in the Fields where they were married. Here his wife removes her wedding ring—and then Cyril solemnly places it on her finger again, just as he did around 40 years ago.

Some people would think this little custom rather pointless and sentimental. Far from it. To the Fletchers it has always meant an annual renewal of their marriage vows. It's rather a lovely idea, isn't it?

WEDNESDAY—FEBRUARY 18.

DO you know why February is shorter than the other months? Well, originally it had 30 days. Then Julius Caesar introduced a reformed calendar and decided to name one of the months after himself—July. As this had only 30 days and he wanted his own month to appear important, he borrowed one day from February. Later, Julius Caesar's nephew, Caesar Augustus, also decided to name a month after himself—August. The same thing happened. Not to be outdone Augustus also borrowed a day from February, reducing it to 28, except in a leap year.

I don't suppose anyone ever gives a thought to those two vain Roman emperors when their months come round. But we can, at least, be thankful to them for reducing the month which seems like the tail-end of winter. I'm always glad when February comes to an end. Another three weeks and it will be the official start of spring!

THURSDAY—FEBRUARY 19.

PATTY was a little American girl whose father was widowed very early in life. He had to bring his daughter up by himself. When she started school her father gave her a ten cent piece, and said: "Keep this dime in your purse always. Any time you need me, call me at the factory. Tell them you want to talk to your dad, and I guarantee they'll let you."

Patty never needed to use that dime but just to know she had it in her purse gave her the confidence and sense of security she needed.

It was a small thing but it's the small things not the big ones that so often give us the courage to keep going.

FRIDAY—FEBRUARY 20.

THE Arabs have this lovely definition of a friend:

" A true friend is one to whom you can tip out all the contents of your heart, chaff and grain together, knowing that the gentlest hands will take and sift it, keep what is worth keeping and with the breath of kindness blow the rest away."

SATURDAY—FEBRUARY 21.

BARBARA MULLEN, the popular actress who won fame as Janet, the housekeeper in the TV series " Dr. Finlay's Casebook," was always genuinely surprised to receive letters of appreciation from viewers all over Britain. The people loved her for the gentle sympathetic character she portrayed week by week. And close friends often said that this talented lady was equally as gracious in ordinary private life.

For all her success, Barbara never forgot her early thwarted ambitions and sharp rebuffs, and that was one reason why she was always ready to lend a helping hand to those, particularly the young, still struggling to win recognition in the world of show-business. None knew better than Barbara that the going can be tough, the pitfalls many. Today there are many people who revere Barbara Mullen's name and cherish her wise counsel.

And it is here that we, in a sense, come in. Whatever our own particular status in life, even if it be quite obscure and humdrum, we can always find opportunities to help somebody worse off than ourselves. Perhaps somebody just around the corner? As the ancient Greek philosopher said, " Kindness often heals terrible wounds."

SUNDAY—FEBRUARY 22.

I WAS an hungered, and ye gave me meat: I was thirsty, and ye gave me drink: I was a stranger, and ye took me in.

MONDAY—FEBRUARY 23.

CALVIN COOLIDGE, the thirtieth President of the United States, was noted for his taciturnity. He rarely wasted a word, but had a dry sense of humour.

One young lady invited to the White House told her father, somewhat rashly, that she was certain she could make Mr Coolidge talk. " All right," said her father. " If he says three words to you I'll give you a fur coat."

When she was introduced to the President, the girl explained what she had said to her father, and confidently awaited the Presidential response. Mr Coolidge sat thoughtfully for a moment, and then said quietly: " Poppa wins ".

He had—by one word!

TUESDAY—FEBRUARY 24.

WHITEWASHED walls,
And old oak beams;
A warming-pan,
A fire that gleams;
A wooden settle,
Wheel-back chairs,
Willow pattern
Plates in pairs—
And there upon
The homespun mat—
Purring lies,
The big white cat!

WEDNESDAY—FEBRUARY 25.

NOEL SCOTT, of Birmingham sent me this message in rhyme which he titles " Helping Hand."

If help is needed, don't delay;
It may be wanted right away;
So volunteer at once, don't wait . . .
Next day—next week—may be too late!

THURSDAY—FEBRUARY 26.

EVERYONE knows the beautiful hymn " Abide With Me." It has brought comfort to innumerable people, especially during some crisis or other in their lives. There was, for instance, Michael, the young vicar of a large parish in the North of England. It was a tough assignment, and, thinking he was making no progress, he grew more and more discouraged. At last he wrote to his bishop to say that he felt that he could no longer continue in the ministry. It was an impossible situation.

Then one day old Mrs Brown, a parishioner, was rushed to hospital for a serious operation. For days her life hung in the balance. Michael visited her regularly, and one afternoon he remarked on her quiet fortitude and tenacity.

Mrs Brown smiled and whispered, " On my bad days I think of the lovely hymn and ask the good Lord to ' abide with me ' all the time. And He does."

Almost in tears Michael clasped the old lady's hand. Her simple words had given him fresh courage and determination never to abandon his flock, however difficult and wayward they might be. He remained in that same parish for close on thirty years.

FRIDAY—FEBRUARY 27.

WHEN Lorna was very young, she and her mother were living in a hotel until their new home was ready. Lorna still remembers an elderly lady with a wheezy chest in a nearby bedroom. Lorna often tapped on the door; she was always made welcome, and was allowed to bounce on the old lady's bed!

One day Lorna's elderly friend hugged her, kissed her, and gave her a tiny bottle of perfume. Lorna did not understand that she was going into hospital, but some instinct told her that she would never see the old lady again.

"Ashes of Roses," the tiny label said. The perfume has long since evaporated, but Lorna still treasures that small bottle as a memento of that early friendship. Whenever she looks at it, the little bottle reminds her that it is never the size of the gift that matters. It is the love that goes with a gift that makes it precious.

SATURDAY—FEBRUARY 28.

I DON'T think you'll find the word "hobrible" in any dictionary. Which is not surprising if I tell you it was coined only the other day by four-year-old Ian.

He had been telling me how another boy, Johnnie, had taken away his favourite model car. I said: "But I always thought you and Johnnie were pals."

"No, we're not, Mr Gay. He used to be nice but now he's just ho . . . ho . . . hobrible."

I think it's a much better word than "horrible," don't you? It's much in use in the Gay household nowadays, when we have to describe something we don't like very much.

LISTENING

It's in the loneliest place
That you sense there's someone near;
It's far from any voices
That the greatest voice you hear.

MARCH

SUNDAY—MARCH 1.

AS cold waters to a thirsty soul, so is good news from a far country.

MONDAY—MARCH 2.

EVERY year at Lytham Methodist Church, Lancashire, the children of the Junior Missionary Association dedicate the money they have collected for work overseas. There is nothing very remarkable about that, of course. You will find busy J.M.A. collectors in many parts of the country.

But at Lytham the children always present the money in little cotton bags—a tradition going back nearly a century, and one which has a most unusual origin. The church at Lytham was founded by a Preston merchant called Hincksman and his wife Dorothy. As a young missionary she had been the sole survivor of a shipwreck in the West Indies. Many years later, after Dorothy had died, her son went out to visit the island on which she had been shipwrecked, and found that some of the cotton dresses she had worn in that hot climate had been lovingly preserved.

When he got back to England he had these clothes made into little collecting bags—and the children of Lytham have kept up this curious custom ever since. I think it's a lovely idea. It reminds them that they are helping to continue the work of a real missionary who risked her life that she might share the Gospel with folk overseas.

TUESDAY—MARCH 3.

ARE you ever tempted to talk at length about your aches and pains? It's good to have a sympathetic ear, but don't forget this profound witticism made by Bert Leston Taylor: "A bore is a man, who, when you ask him how he is, tells you."

WEDNESDAY—MARCH 4.

HOW strong is your faith today? It does so vary, doesn't it? Depending on all sorts of personal circumstances at any particular time. That is why I like the definition which C. S. Lewis once gave of faith. In his view it was "the art of holding on to what your reason has once accepted—in spite of your changing moods."

So, hold on! You may be feeling a bit low today, but cling to your beliefs in spite of the ups and downs. Tomorrow—or one day soon—you will be so much more cheerful you will wonder how you could ever have had doubts!

THURSDAY—MARCH 5.

DID you know that the most important person in the country—apart from Royalty, that is—has no key to the front door? There isn't even a keyhole in the famous door of No. 10 Downing Street. It may be nice for it to be opened automatically as soon as the Prime Minister arrives home, but it is an important reminder that while in office the top person in the land has no real home or proper privacy. He—or she—does not even possess a key to the front door. As we read in the New Testament, "He that is greatest among you shall be your servant."

FRIDAY—MARCH 6.

WHEN my niece Joanna was about five years old she asked me if there would be dolls to play with in heaven.

" I shouldn't think so," I replied cautiously.

" Then I must play with Susan all I can now," Joanna declared. And right away she wheeled in her dolls' pram and was soon busy tucking her favourite doll under a little sheet and blanket.

As I watched Joanna I thought how wise she was to play with her doll while she could. She had already learned the importance of doing things now. We all have a tendency to put things off until tomorrow. *Today* is the best time to speak to a lonely neighbour, change library books for a housebound friend and offer sympathy to the widower who lives round the corner.

SATURDAY—MARCH 7.

QUAINT little Fowey in Cornwall is well known to thousands of people who visit it every year. The town is proud to number amongst its sons the name of Sir Arthur Quiller Couch who died in 1944. Sir Arthur's father was the local doctor, but Arthur did not follow in father's footsteps. Instead he turned to literature and became a celebrated writer. A number of his books have been used as text books in schools.

If you visit Fowey you will see a large granite monument on the hillside overlooking the harbour, placed there in memory of this famous son of the town. The inscription reads:—

" Courteous in manner, charitable in judgment, chivalrous in action, he manifested in life, as in literature, the dignity of manhood, the sanctity of home, and the sovereignty of God."

SUNDAY—MARCH 8.

LET your light so shine before men, that they may see your good works, and glorify your Father which is in heaven.

MONDAY—MARCH 9.

HOBBIES are fine things if they do not run away with you. For example, I know a keen angler who can no longer find time to fish because he is Secretary of the local Anglers' Club and all his spare time is taken up in working for it.

It is sometimes a sad fact that a Christian can no longer find time to be a committed Christian because of religious duties! It's a paradox, but true.

Then there are the people who put their hobbies before their work, their friends and even their families. We have all met the bore who can talk about nothing else except the bee in his bonnet.

We all should keep a rein on our hobbies so that they do not turn into hobby-horses and gallop off with us!

TUESDAY—MARCH 10.

I DON'T know who the wise man was who described a home in these words: " A place in which we are wanted, in which there is someone to whom we matter more than anything in the world, of such a place are the four walls made. But to cover them with garlands we ourselves must love."

The poet Goethe said, " He is happiest, be he king or peasant, who finds peace in his home."

WEDNESDAY—MARCH 11.

A HUNDRED years ago Bishop William Stubbs was one of the foremost historians of the Anglican Church, and did a great deal to promote the study of English constitutional history.

He once said that he had only three rules in life: one was never to do anything underhand; the second was never to get his feet wet; and the third was to be in bed by ten.

Simple rules—but very sensible ones!

THURSDAY—MARCH 12.

RECENTLY I watched a pair of blackbirds building a nest in my garden. They used dried grasses and leaves and even some of my garden twine — which I didn't begrudge! — working tirelessly until the masterpiece was finished.

As I watched from the window I almost envied their skill until I half recalled some words penned by John Ruskin, the Victorian writer and critic. I turned to my bookcase to refresh my memory, and here they are:

> "Make yourselves nests of pleasant thoughts. None of us yet know, for none of us have been taught in early youth, what fairy palaces we may build of beautiful thought—a proof against all adversity. Bright fancies, satisfied memories, noble histories, faithful sayings, treasure-houses of precious and restful thoughts, which care cannot disturb, nor pain make gloomy, nor poverty take away from us—houses built without hands, for our souls to live in."

As I closed the book I thought, if I can only do that, I, too, will be a worthy nest-builder.

FRIDAY—MARCH 13.

THE things children say . . .

A very well-known, but aged person, had just died, and the usual mark of respect was shown by all flags being flown at half-mast. " I wonder why they always do that?" queried one neighbour to another, who also admitted that she wasn't quite sure. However, the second neighbour's ten-year-old daughter thought she knew. " It will be because they are not quite sure whether they have gone up above—or down below!"

SATURDAY—MARCH 14.

YOU may have come across one of the many books written by André Maurois. This French author achieved fame both in France and Britain.

He was forced to leave his homeland when the Nazis occupied France. He also suffered family setbacks. Yet, looking back, he was able to write these comforting words:

" Misfortune has taught me that sacrifice, when it is unmixed with pride, gives man incomparable joys. In fact, the greatest happiness of my life, the brief moments of ecstasy and rapture, have been those when I was delivered, through love or charity, from vain considerations of myself. To forget oneself is wonderful and in humility there is immense security. Seated in the lowest place I can never be deposed."

Great and wise words.

SUNDAY—MARCH 15.

TO every thing there is a season, and a time to every purpose under the heaven.

MONDAY—MARCH 16.

POETS' CORNER in Westminster Abbey commemorates many famous people, but only one Australian—the 19th-century poet Adam Lindsay Gordon, whose best-known lines hold a message for today as certainly as they did when first written:

Question not, but live and labour
Till yon goal be won,
Helping every feeble neighbour,
Seeking help from none;
Life is mostly froth and bubble,
Two things only stand like stone:
—Kindness in another's trouble,
Courage in your own.

TUESDAY—MARCH 17.

WE'VE all heard it said, by folk who are not very fussy about their appearance: " Oh, it's not how we look but what we are that matters."

Well, James Galway, that master of the flute who has often delighted us on TV, has something to say about that. One day the conductor of Sadler's Wells Orchestra said to his players:

" It's time we stopped being so lax. For example, members of the orchestra turn up unshaven. They look sloppy and think sloppy."

" I understood what he was getting at," writes Galway in his autobiography. " I know an old lady in Belfast who is 75, yet if she only goes to buy some potatoes in the morning, she puts on earrings and good hat and manages to look terrific and everybody feels better for meeting her."

I haven't met that old lady—but how I would like to!

THE GIFT

WEDNESDAY—MARCH 18.

MY friend Bruce, who used to be a Welfare Officer, often visited an elderly man called Sam, who lived in a dingy tenement. Sam was almost bed-ridden and often in pain, but he always had a cheery smile for Bruce.

"Has anyone besides me called this week?" Bruce once asked him.

"Yes, God got here first," Sam replied.

Seeing Bruce's puzzled expression, Sam pointed a gnarled finger towards the window-sill. There, just at the point where a shaft of sunlight glinted through the dusty window, two crocuses bloomed in a chipped pot.

THURSDAY—MARCH 19.

ARTHUR MARSHALL, journalist and radio personality, was once asked in a television interview what he liked about village life. He lives in the countryside a few miles from Exeter and he replied to the question by describing what once happened during a power-cut. "Half the village still had electricity," he explained. "And they looked across to see the other half in total darkness." Immediately the villagers with lights set to work to prepare hot soup, cakes and anything else which might help, and then took the supplies across to the houses in darkness. "I don't think," he added, "that's the sort of thing you'd get in a big city."

Arthur Marshall was probably right, but all the same there's no real reason why the community spirit, so typical of a little village, should not be extended to any neighbourhood, is there? It all depends on how neighbourly you and I are willing to be.

FRIDAY—MARCH 20.

SHE lay alone and ill last week,
When in came little Sue.
" I've brought some flowers, Gran," she said,
" With love from me to you."
Three crumpled daffodils—and yet
They made a sad heart sing,
And Gran gave thanks for all the wealth
A child's love can bring.

SATURDAY—MARCH 21.

WHILE on holiday in Christchurch, I visited the ancient priory and gazed in awe at the magnificent architecture, stained glass windows, superb sculpture and wood carvings. The skill of the craftsmen who had laboured centuries ago amazed me. I could not help but wonder, as I looked up at the vaulted ceiling and massive pillars, how many men had worked, and for how long, to complete such a majestic building.

And then depression gripped me. Anything that I could do appeared paltry by comparison. I was still preoccupied when a frail old lady with a bent back approached a brass lectern nearby. With gnarled, care-worn hands she polished the wide-spread eagles' wings, then slowly worked her way down to the base.

I asked how often she polished the lectern and she told me she had done it almost every week for the past sixty years.

Sixty years! I pictured her, perhaps as a young wife and mother, busy with her tin of polish, year after year. Her devotion lifted my spirits and I realised I had been wrong to feel depressed. It is not so much what we can do that matters, but the dedication with which we do it.

SUNDAY—MARCH 22.

THOU hast delivered my soul from death, mine eyes from tears, and my feet from falling.

MONDAY—MARCH 23.

YOU'VE got to hand it to Elaine Dale for courage. She has a severe physical handicap, but in spite of this she learned to type and earn her own living, met a handsome young man and married him, and now has a lovely little girl, intact to the shell-pink tips of her finger nails.

What is more, Elaine Dale is looking after the child herself—with her toes. For Elaine Dale was a thalidomide baby born without any arms.

The foot that rocks that cradle should leave an imprint on the world.

TUESDAY—MARCH 24.

MY little nephew Brian limped tearfully home with badly grazed knees. His mother washed them gently and soon Brian was watching "Jackanory" on the television, his painful knees forgotten.

At bedtime his mother asked him what he would like to thank God for before lying down.

"For my sore knees," Brian replied promptly.

"Why your knees?" asked his surprised mother.

"'Cos now I can watch God making them better," Brian replied.

When I heard about this I thought how much happier we would be if our faith were more childlike. We rarely give thanks for life's hard times and yet it is through them that we gain fresh strength, wisdom and courage.

WEDNESDAY—MARCH 25.

THE other day I came across the following facts about the human body. We have an average of 20 square feet of skin, with up to 5 million hairs. We have 650 muscles, 206 bones, 100 joints, 60,000 miles of arteries, veins and capillaries—and 13,000 million nerve cells! Our blood contains about two billion red cells to carry oxygen to our tissues and about 3000 million white cells to fight disease . . .

When I read facts like these, I simply echo the words of the psalmist who exclaimed " Behold, I am fearfully and wonderfully made!" (Psalm 139). Even in those far-off days that writer had a sense of wonder. In our scientific age how much more should we stand in awe before the marvels of the body!

THURSDAY—MARCH 26.

ABRAHAM LINCOLN, the well-loved American President, was sometimes called the Great Emancipator because of his courageous, outspoken fight for the freedom of slaves.

This compassionate, God-fearing statesman was assassinated in his mid-fifties but his name lives on. His home in Springfield, Illinois, is a national shrine. One night a few years ago a young mother was passing the house with her small son.

" Look, Mamma," the child exclaimed, " Abraham Lincoln has left his lights on."

When I heard this it reminded me of something Jesus once said: " Let your light so shine before men that they may see your good works."

It's something we should all try to do, isn't it? Even if our little candle does flicker at times!

FRIDAY—MARCH 27.

FEW things can be more miserable than being caught out in the open when it starts to rain—particularly if you're walking or cycling and perhaps not quite clad for it. Two people who often felt sorry for folk caught in a downpour were Mrs Dent and her daughter Dorothy who lived in the village of Elsdon, Northumberland. On rainy days they used to watch for passers-by and invite them into their cottage for a cup of tea and a slice of home-made cake.

Dorothy and her mother have both passed on now, but the people who were once glad of their kindness have made sure they are not forgotten. If you ever go to Elsdon you will see a seat near the church, placed there in grateful memory of the two ladies who, for 44 years, sheltered strangers caught in the rain.

SATURDAY—MARCH 28.

A BIRD on a tree . . . it's something we have all seen a thousand times. But then, happily, most of us haven't had the handicap of Sheila Hocken.

Sheila was born blind, but, after many years, had her sight restored. From that wonderful day her life became one of endless discovery—as when she looked out of the window and saw for the first time not only a tree but a bird sitting on a branch. In her delight she called her husband to share in this marvel.

" It's just a bird on a tree," he said.

And so it was. But how much more life has to offer when we view the everyday wonders around us with the same joy with which Sheila Hocken saw her first bird on a branch.

SUNDAY—MARCH 29.

THE Lord watch between thee and me, when we are absent one from another.

MONDAY—MARCH 30.

HAVE you ever thought how much happiness depends on the way other people behave towards you? If someone in the family grumbles over the breakfast table, the day gets off to a bad start, doesn't it?

If the postman fails to bring the letter you expected from your special friend, then your spirits sink further. It then only takes a neighbour to tell you how ill you look, for your spirits to plummet altogether. What a difference if you had been told that you were looking great today!

We do well to remember that all this works the other way round as well. Do you and I add to or subtract from other people's gladness? Whether a day will bring us more or less joy is largely beyond our power to control, but whether we *give* happiness or not does rest with ourselves.

TUESDAY—MARCH 31.

A CERTAIN social worker took his work very seriously. He was particularly concerned about the problem of leisure for people retiring after a lifetime of work. One day he went to see a farm worker who was soon to retire. He frowned when he came on him leaning on a gate gazing at the fields and woods.

"Don't you think you should have a hobby for when you retire?" the social worker asked.

"What do you think this is?" the farm worker replied, while continuing to lean and gaze.

APRIL

WEDNESDAY—APRIL 1.

AT the age of 60, when most professional ladies are thinking of a quiet retirement, one retired nurse took on a new family.

Eve Osborn had been a nurse in Uganda where she looked after abandoned children. When the time came for her to retire to England everyone expected her to go alone. She didn't—she brought two-year-old orphaned triplets with her. It wasn't easy—there were all sorts of formalities to be gone through, but in the end she won the right to bring them home to share her retirement in Ilfracombe, Devon. And as if that wasn't enough she acquired another two girls who had been left in care, and she became mother to them, too.

So today I salute the great good heart of Eve Osborn.

THURSDAY—APRIL 2.

WHERE the church notices should have been somebody had written up the following, which attracted my attention and caught the eye of several passers-by:

Check list
Cancel the milk
Cancel the newspapers
Arrange for cat to be fed
Buy sun-glasses, sun-tan lotion
Thank God for holidays.

I wonder if we do sufficiently thank God for these happy times of physical and spiritual refreshment. Thank God for holidays!

LEARNING

Bless't be the hands,
Gentle, caring,
That teach a child
The joy of sharing.

FRIDAY—APRIL 3.

THE other day I did something I had not done for years—I pulled a wishbone. It was my small niece who persuaded me to do it and, of course, she was thrilled when it broke and she was left with the larger part and therefore the wish.

Of course it was just a bit of fun, but it brought back memories to me, particularly of an elderly relative I knew as a child. When I pulled a wishbone with him he said to me, " I'm glad you got the wish but remember—never put your wishbone where your backbone ought to be."

I don't think I understood him then, but I do now. And so will my little niece some day, for I passed on the old man's piece of wisdom to her, too. And now you've got it as well!

SATURDAY—APRIL 4.

HAVE you ever heard of William Shockley? Or John Bardeen? Or Walter Brattain? I'm afraid I hadn't. But these three Americans were awarded the Nobel Prize in 1947 for their invention of the first transistor—the tiny semiconductor which has replaced the valve and revolutionised radio, television, hi-fi and all communication systems. They were working for the Bell Telephone laboratories, trying to improve the efficiency of exchanges, when they hit on their brilliant idea.

Just another example of how something so important in our lives—the amazing little transistor—is rather taken for granted, and its inventors forgotten. Still, why should I be surprised? After all, nobody ever troubled to record the name of the genius who first invented the wheel!

SUNDAY—APRIL 5.

GREAT is truth, and mighty above all things.

MONDAY—APRIL 6.

INNOCENCE is bliss. And perhaps bliss is innocence.

I'm thinking of little Robert, not long started doing sums at school.

"Do you like your teacher?" his mother asked.

"Oh, yes," was the reply, "and she likes me."

"How do you know that?"

"Because she puts kisses all over my homework!"

TUESDAY—APRIL 7.

HAVE you ever come across this little poem by Robert Heywood? Its title is "By Degrees":

One step upon another,
And the longest walk is ended;
One stitch upon another,
And the largest rent is mended;
One brick upon another,
And the highest wall is made;
One flake upon another,
And the deepest snow is laid.

Then do not look disheartened
On the work you have to do,
And say that such a mighty task
You never can get through.
But just endeavour day by day
Another point to gain;
And soon the mountain which you fear
Will prove to be a plain.

WEDNESDAY—APRIL 8.

I WAS looking through a pile of odds and ends at a Scout jumble sale when I happened to pick up a little framed picture of a charming old house. Just as I was about to return it to the pile my attention was caught by some wording on it:

"Home—where we are treated best but grumble the most."

I confess I put it back on the pile—but I think the Lady of the House was a little surprised at how helpful I was when I got home that afternoon!

THURSDAY—APRIL 9.

LORNA was telling me about a boat trip she had made by sea to the River Dart in Devon. At first the waves were playfully choppy but soon the sky darkened and the water became a boiling cauldron of fury. The boat tossed like a cork and poor Lorna felt quite seasick.

"But suddenly everything changed," she told me. "The boat nosed its way up the Dart and we were soon in calmer water. It was marvellous!"

Thinking over Lorna's experience, it struck me how often life is like that. It takes some rough water to make us appreciate calmer days. We grumble at the boredom of daily routine but when trouble comes we sigh for the tranquillity of that routine!

I have resolved to look about more carefully the next time life seems dull. I intend to enjoy the scent of a rose and the song of a bird. If I also remember to show friendship to my lonely neighbour and to thank God for His fresh air and sunshine, I suspect that dreariness will go from days that I would otherwise have called dull!

FRIDAY—APRIL 10.

TROUBLES don't seem half so grim
With someone by your side;
Someone who can help you and
In whom you can confide.
If we helped other folk whose lives
Are maybe drab and grey,
Just think how we could brighten up
This sad old world today!

SATURDAY—APRIL 11.

THE rector of a certain parish in Lanarkshire had for months been trying unsuccessfully to persuade his people to attend Sunday morning service more regularly. Various excuses were given for non-attendance, although all the parishioners, without exception, firmly declared that they really loved their local church; it was part of their very lives.

One Sunday morning the rector mounted the steps of his pulpit as usual and gazed around. He noted many empty pews—fewer worshippers than ever. Then he leaned forward, smiled at the sparse congregation and remarked: "There is a saying—Absence makes the heart grow fonder. All I want to say today is that this lovely church of ours must indeed have a number of staunch friends. Just look around!"

Thereafter the Sunday morning attendances improved noticeably.

SUNDAY—APRIL 12.

HE shall feed his flock like a shepherd: he shall gather the lambs with his arm, and carry them in his bosom.

MONDAY—APRIL 13.

DO you remember the shoe firm that used to advertise widely with the slogan " We are at your feet "? It was a clever play on words but nevertheless it did suggest that the firm was entirely at its customers' service.

On the evening before the crucifixion, Jesus took a basin and towel and washed His disciples' feet. By this lowly, loving act He demonstrated that He came into the world to serve and not to be served—then gently told His disciples to serve and care for one another with equal love and humility.

The thought uppermost in my mind this Easter is: what a wonderful world it would be if everyone really took to heart the lesson that Jesus taught us. And when I say everyone that, of course, includes me!

TUESDAY—APRIL 14.

"THE STORMY ROAD " was the first book to be written by Gertrude Phillipson. Nothing specially remarkable about that, you might say. But her publishers thought she was remarkable—because the book was published on the author's 100th birthday! She had not even started to write it till she was 91.

The foreword was by the well-known author George Sava, who wrote many books himself. Not only did he express the hope that he would be able to write the introduction to her second novel in due course, he stated what so many people believe to be true: " Life does not begin or stop at any age. It goes on from our first day to our last, and Gertrude Phillipson has showed us the way of enjoying it to the full."

THE GOOD WAY

Through the years the pace of life grows slower,
We know our time on earth is only lent;
Let's make a vow to spend each moment wisely,
And peace of mind will bring its own content.

WEDNESDAY—APRIL 15.

IT'S very easy to get a little too big for our boots, to imagine that we're indispensable. Here are a few lines that suggest how far "off the beam" our estimate can be. I don't know who wrote them. I imagine they have travelled so far that I may never know.

Some time when you feel your going
Will leave an unfillable hole,
Just follow this simple example
And see how it humbles your soul;
Take a bucket and fill it with water,
Put your hands in it up to the wrists,
Pull them out and the hole that remains
Will show how much you'll be missed!

THURSDAY—APRIL 16.

ONE of our treasured family possessions is a collection of four tiny silver coins—genuine Maundy Money presented some years ago by the Queen to a distant relation. Every year it is the royal custom to present these specially-minted coins "to as many old men and as many old women as the Sovereign is years of age."

The Maundy Thursday ceremony, usually performed in Westminster Abbey, is a tradition which stretches back to the time when Jesus washed his disciples' feet at the Last Supper—a sign that they were to love each other in the way that He loved and gave Himself for them. "Greater love hath no man than this that a man lay down his life for his friends."

I think we often forget that Holy Week—no less than Christmas—is the time for giving . . . whether it is Maundy Money or a simple act of service for our fellow-men.

FRIDAY—APRIL 17.

EVERY Good Friday millions all over the world sing the well-loved hymn which begins:

There is a green hill far away,
Without a city wall,
Where the dear Lord was crucified
Who died to save us all.

We might expect this great hymn, which deals so movingly with the atoning death of Christ, to have been written by some theologian. It was, in fact, written by an Irish lady with a life-long devotion to children, Mrs Cecil Frances Alexander.

Many of her hymns were for her Sunday School classes, but this one was written at the bedside of a little girl who was dangerously ill. The child recovered and ever afterwards regarded this hymn as her very own.

The French composer Gounod once described it as the most perfect hymn in the English language, and wrote his own setting for it, sending an autographed copy to Mrs Alexander. The tune we nearly always use today was composed by William Horsley in 1844—a simple melody appropriate to the words. Together they powerfully convey the solemn yet peaceful atmosphere of Good Friday.

SATURDAY—APRIL 18.

THE writer Thomas Paine once said, " Reputation is what the world thinks of us. Character is what God and angels know of us."

SUNDAY—APRIL 19.

I KNOW that my redeemer liveth, and that he shall stand at the latter day upon the earth.

MONDAY—APRIL 20.

NOW when the jonquil white
In gladness springs
From earth which yesterday
In frozen bondage lay,
And from the budding bough,
A blackbird sings,
Remember the tomb,
The stone that rolled away
On that first Easter morn
When hope was born.
And fill the world with praise;
Love conquers all today!

TUESDAY—APRIL 21.

FOUR-YEAR-OLD Allan had just received a most important picture from his Gran. When she was staying with them she had taken a photograph of his two much-loved pussies playing on an armchair.

The first thing Allan did was to carry the photograph to his pussies, half-asleep on that very chair. To his surprise they were not at all interested.

" Come on," he begged them. " It's you. Look at it!"

His voice brought one of the pussies to life and as Allan held the picture in front of it it began to purr.

Allan was delighted. He jumped to his feet and raced to Mummy in the kitchen.

" Mummy," he shouted, " Crispy's seen the picture and he likes it!"

What a lovely world young children live in, when humans and animals are all part of one great harmony!

WEDNESDAY—APRIL 22.

LIKE many other people the Lady of the House and I always try, every Easter, to go to a live performance of Handel's *Messiah.* The stirring music never fails to move us with its beauty and majesty. When I mentioned this to our church organist he asked me how observant I was. Had I ever noticed, for instance, in which part of the Messiah the highest note occurs?

I hadn't. But I guessed that it would be in one of the great choruses, such as " And the Glory of the Lord," or maybe the magnificent " Hallelujah " chorus itself.

" No," smiled my friend. And he told me that the most exalted note of all occurs in the lovely air, " I know that my Redeemer liveth," and is reached on the word " risen ". The more you think about it, the more you come to realise it was not put there by mere chance. For Handel knew that this one word is the secret of the Easter miracle which proclaims its immortal message to us all.

THURSDAY—APRIL 23.

SOME of you will, I hope, still remember the name of Professor Gordon Hamilton Fairley, the cancer expert who was killed by a bomb a few years ago. His widow, Daphne, declared afterwards that she felt no trace of bitterness. She went on: " We, as a family and friends, pray that we will learn something invaluable from our loss. If you want to do something—do it today. Say sorry: show somebody you love them now. If you had a row—make it up. Don't waste time. We never did."

Brave and wise words from a very gallant lady.

THE DEEP

Man may often subdue the land
And fashion it to his ends,
But over the tumbling, broiling waves
A mightier power extends.

FRIDAY—APRIL 24.

ALMOST everybody has heard of Mother Theresa who works in the slums of Calcutta. Less well-known is Major Gardiner, who also works in that teeming city. Having retired from the army after 36 years of service, the major looked round for some way of helping his fellow-men. For 20 years he has been providing the poor folk of Calcutta with one square meal a day. Thousands come to his efficiently run Feeding Centre each lunch-time, and in the evening he sets off into the darkest slums in search of those who would otherwise starve.

Major Gardiner cheerfully carries out this selfless work seven days a week. Most of us think of retirement as a time when we will sit back and enjoy a well-earned rest. Not so this remarkable soldier—still on active service for his Lord.

SATURDAY—APRIL 25.

DO-IT-YOURSELF is not my strong point when it comes to hammers and nails, so when we needed a small bookcase for the fireside recess, I took the measurements along to a carpenter's workshop.

The foreman frowned at my piece of paper then shook his head. Polite but regretful, he explained that he could not oblige. The bookcase was only a " one-off " and he could not spare a man from his assembly line to make it.

As I thought about this afterwards, I was glad that God has no such system. We are all " one-offs " and He cares for us individually. Each of us has his or her special place in the world, where we can do our best with the talents that He has given us.

SUNDAY—APRIL 26.

THEREFORE all things whatsoever ye would that men should do to you, do ye even so to them.

MONDAY—APRIL 27.

A SCHOOL teacher friend was sitting in his garden, reading through a pile of compositions from his class of nine-year-olds when I happened to pass.

"Come and read this," he called.

His class had been asked to write an imaginary piece on "How I went to America." Some said they had gone by steamer and some by plane, but one boy had other ideas.

"I set out to swim," he wrote, "but the sea was very rough. When I got half way across I could go no further. So I just had to turn and swim back. It was too far to swim to America."

It reminded me of the boy who wrote what is claimed to be the shortest autobiography ever written—the autobiography of a chicken: "I died in my shell."

TUESDAY—APRIL 28.

A LANCASHIRE man and his wife were out walking one day when he noticed a gas bill lying on the footpath. He picked it up, took a good look at it, turned to his wife and said, "I'm going to pay this 'ere bill, Maggie."

"Whatever do you want to do that for, you soft thing," she protested. "It isn't yours."

"No," he replied, "but there's sixty-four pence discount, and I might as well have it as anyone else!"

WEDNESDAY—APRIL 29.

ARTHUR is a retired minister who very recently lost his wife. I called to see him, wondering what I could find to say that might bring him some comfort. I need not have worried. He welcomed me in with his usual cheerful courtesy.

"Of course, I miss her very much," he said, "and sometimes feel very lonely. But I'm thankful for two things. The first is that the faith which helped me to console others during my ministry is now a great comfort to me. The second is that after bereavement people are so kind, so very kind."

I left feeling quite uplifted, thankful, like Arthur, for the double strength of faith and friendship.

THURSDAY—APRIL 30.

IF you have ever looked at armour in a museum you may have thought, as I used to do, that our ancestors were much smaller than we are. This is apparently not so. When the armour was worn the plates were more widely separated, and the way the suits of armour are displayed makes them look misleadingly small. Research has, in fact, shown that some of our ancestors, old Stone Age Man, for example, were actually taller than modern man.

I must admit that I was rather pleased to learn this. You see, I have always felt that it is wrong to think of ourselves as superior to the generations who have gone before. We have all kinds of advantages over the people of the past—yet we are fundamentally just like them. Human nature is the same the world over—and throughout history.

THE DISTANT VIEW

Looking through the glasses
You see miles and miles away,
Catch snow on far-off passes,
A steamer in the bay.
Then when you're sitting quietly, a cosy fire close by,
You can summon up the picture in imagination's eye.

MAY

FRIDAY—MAY 1.

SOME of the world's greatest thinkers have been devoutly religious men. Take, for example, one of the founders of modern astronomy, Johann Kepler, of Prague. When he had completed his monumental task of working out the laws which control the movement of planets he remarked that he felt as though he had been "thinking God's thoughts after Him."

Kepler died in 1630, but many a recent scientist has been just as reverent and humble in his research, and shown that there is no conflict between science and real religion.

SATURDAY—MAY 2.

IN Scripture lessons at school our teacher would sometimes bring out a Hebrew Bible. "Can you read it, sir?" would be the chorus that greeted it. He would read a few lines of what seemed strange sounds to us, but his real object in bringing out the Bible was not to show off his knowledge of Hebrew.

"Look, boys," he would say, opening it up at what seemed to us to be the end of the book. "In a Hebrew Bible what seems to us to be the back of the book is the front; the end is the beginning!"

"The end is the beginning . . ." that's true of life, isn't it? Work ends and holidays start. Holidays end and work starts again. Bachelordom ends and married life begins. Retirement comes and a new phase of life opens up. Even death itself is not an end, but a beginning.

SUNDAY—MAY 3.

WITH God all things are possible.

MONDAY—MAY 4.

HOWARD C. HOEFLICH of Miami, Florida, is a good friend of *The Friendship Book.* He wrote to me recently and, as usual, it was of other people he was thinking. " I hope," he wrote, " I can still be of some use to my friends and family."

Why do I mention this? Well, because at the time Mr Hoeflich was just coming up to his 98th birthday!

This amazing man went on, " If I had known I was going to live this long I would have taken better care of myself!"

TUESDAY—MAY 5.

I DON'T know if children in school still have to learn by heart long passages from the Bible like we did. But I do know that, as the years pass, a long-remembered passage or text can be a great comfort. Others of my generation are the same. Take my friend Allan, for instance, who recently came out of hospital after a serious operation. A frightening experience? Not at all. He told me, " I never worried. I just kept saying to myself, 'Beneath me are the everlasting arms,' And I knew that whatever happened I wasn't alone."

Alexander Whyte, a famous Scottish minister of last century, often concluded a household visit by quoting a well-known verse and saying: " Put that under your tongue and suck it like a sweetie."

I know what he meant, and I'm sure you do, too.

FREEDOM

Who does not love
Sometimes to say
Goodbye to things
Of every day?

Welcome to paths
By tumbling streams
Where we may wander
With our dreams.

WEDNESDAY—MAY 6.

MIRIAM EKER of Longsight, Manchester, sent me these lines which she calls " The Haven "

Home is such a cosy word, made up of letters four,
And oh, the satisfaction when your key turns in the door!
The chairs, the table, walls and hearth, these are your own to touch,
No matter if they're shabby, they mean so very much;
Whether you've a stately home for which some people yearn,
Or whether it's a tiny place with not much room to turn,
Home's a blessed haven, it holds the very core,
And the secret of your pleasure, when your key turns in the door.

THURSDAY—MAY 7.

DOES it surprise you to learn that John Wesley constantly urged his Methodist followers to think about making money? " Gain all you can," he would say. " And save all you can." But he always added a third instruction which made all the difference: " When you have done that, then *give* all you can."

FRIDAY—MAY 8.

THE Irish do provide us with plenty of innocent humour, don't they? I like this specimen which a tourist apparently found pinned up on a monastery notice board:

" There will be a procession next Sunday afternoon in the grounds of the monastery. If it rains in the afternoon the procession will take place in the morning."

SATURDAY—MAY 9.

IF you are buying rose bushes for your garden how do you choose them? For scent? For colour?

The Lady of the House has no doubts. "Always buy your roses after a shower of rain," she says.

That way you can tell the ones that are going to look bravely up from their stems, come sunshine or shower and those that will droop in a bad summer.

It's a bit like life, isn't it? When trouble comes along, we soon find who our true friends are.

SUNDAY—MAY 10.

THE fear of the Lord is the beginning of wisdom.

MONDAY—MAY 11.

MARION was widowed early in life—a terrible experience, for she and her husband had been very close. She told me afterwards that the moment she dreaded most was when she and her small son Trevor would leave the house in which the three had been so happy, but which could no longer be her home. It was all she could do not to break down as, gripping Trevor's hand, she opened the door to pass through it for the last time.

As she fumbled to close it behind her, Trevor exclaimed, "Look, Mummy—God's sky is still there. It's coming with us!"

It was the turning point for them both. From that moment Marion knew that she could go on and build a new life for herself—and her son.

TUESDAY—MAY 12.

I KNOW a comprehensive school which is so big that there are 200 in Sixth Form. And every year when the Christmas season comes round these Sixth Formers go into the town, round up about 200 pensioners and give them a party.

The young folk arrange everything—transport, food, games, entertainment—and it doesn't cost the guests a penny. The old folk appreciate it tremendously, not because it's a free treat, but because many of them are lonely and housebound. They really enjoy the companionship of young people and are glad to see just how much good there is in the much-maligned youth of today.

WEDNESDAY—MAY 13.

I HAVE been reading once again one of my favourite 18th century poems—and one, I am sure, which will remain a much-loved classic for generations to come. I refer to the "Elegy written in a Country Churchyard" by Thomas Gray. Based on the poet's meditation in the little churchyard of Stoke Poges, Buckinghamshire, it describes in flawless verse his thoughts on the forgotten graves of humble countryfolk. I particularly like his picture of the contentment which they enjoyed, poor though they were:

Far from the madding crowd's ignoble strife
Their sober wishes never learnt to stray;
Along the cool, sequestered vale of life
They kept the noiseless tenor of their way.

I think that if he were still alive, Thomas Gray would still be singing the praises of a quiet life—even more so, perhaps, in our busy, noisy 1980's!

BEAUTY

Since Adam was driven from Eden
Mankind has been counting the cost,
And that's why we love to have gardens
That mirror the beauty we lost.

THURSDAY—MAY 14.

HAVE you heard of the statue of Christ that stands in the Cathedral Church of Copenhagen? Much larger than life, it was the work of Bertel A. Thorvaldsen, who was acclaimed as the most eminent sculptor of his time. It stands with arms outstretched in invitation: " Come unto Me and I will give you rest."

A remarkable work, but here is the most remarkable thing of all about it: it is only possible to see this Christ when kneeling at His feet. Before you see His face you must bend your knees to Him.

FRIDAY—MAY 15.

GREAT people often have a quality of humility that is lacking in ordinary mortals. I am thinking today of the world-famous pianist, Paderewski, who was born in 1860 and became the Prime Minister of Poland. Once he visited the house in Bonn that is the birthplace of the composer Beethoven. The house had become a museum with many relics of the composer, including his piano.

Years later a group of students were being shown round Beethoven's home when one asked if he might play Beethoven's piano. The guide permitted him to do so. The student sat down and played a passage from one of Beethoven's piano sonatas and he played extremely well.

When the student learned that Paderewski had also visited the house he asked if he, too, had played Beethoven's piano.

" No," said the guide. " He was invited to, but he wouldn't because he said he was unworthy to play the great musician's piano."

SATURDAY—MAY 16.

I WAS amused to hear about the schoolteacher who was supervising meals and noticed a five-year-old newcomer eat his dinner, then join the queue for a second time. Knowing that there was plenty food, she said nothing, but when she saw him join the queue for a third time, she went over and took him aside.

Before she could say a word, Jimmy burst into tears: "My muvver said I was to have free dinners—*and I can only manage two!*"

SUNDAY—MAY 17.

FROM the rising of the sun unto the going down of the same the Lord's name is to be praised.

MONDAY—MAY 18.

THE Rev. Dr William Barclay, who died in the early part of 1978, was well known for his writings on the Bible and early Christianity. He was a gifted speaker, too, who entranced and held an audience by the simplicity of his teaching.

How did he manage it all? The secret, he confessed, was that he worked by night as well as day. He needed little sleep and, from his student days, would rise at about two o'clock in the morning, work for two or three hours and then return to bed, to get up again refreshed at breakfast time.

He worked and spoke in public under the handicap of being almost totally deaf. It was a handicap he overcame so successfully that he was able to train and conduct the choir of Trinity College, Glasgow, where he was professor.

He left behind an inspiration and an example for us all.

DREAMING

Far from city street
With myriad passing faces
The sweetest thoughts dwell
In green secret places.

TUESDAY—MAY 19.

TO stand beside you when you're down,
No matter what folks say,
To help you find the sun again,
When skies are black and grey,
To share a cheery word or two
To give when there is need,
If we can do this cheerfully
We'll be true friends indeed.

WEDNESDAY—MAY 20.

VAL DOONICAN, the famous Irish entertainer, started life in the humblest of circumstances, the youngest of eight children. As a boy he was taken to hospital with scarlet fever. On one visit his father asked him to write down something he would dearly love to have when he came out of hospital.

Val knew that his father was too poor to buy anything, but that he was very clever with his hands. So he asked for a "trolley" or "bogey"—one of those little carts made from planks and pram-wheels.

When he came out of hospital the first thing he saw on entering the front room was a marvellous little "car" complete with steering wheel, which his father had made. But there was a strict condition attached. He must never ride on the pavement, where it might be a danger to pedestrians.

One day young Val broke this rule. When his father found out he calmly took the vehicle to pieces and hung the wheels up in the yard! And now his son looks back and admires his father, just as much for his caring discipline as for his generosity and kindness.

THURSDAY—MAY 21.

YOU could say that Samuel Plimsoll left his mark.

He was the Member of Parliament for Derby and he found out that many accidents and sinkings at sea were caused by vessels being overloaded.

But how could the authorities know if a ship was carrying too much cargo? Plimsoll hit on the idea of a line painted on the hull of every ship. If that was submerged the ship was unsafe and should not go out to sea.

No one will ever be able to tell how many lives the Plimsoll Line or Mark saved—and still saves. Next time you notice the mark, say a silent word of thanks to the "Sailors' Friend," the ex-clerk from Sheffield who cared about the lives of others.

FRIDAY—MAY 22.

SOME adults were looking over the fence of a playing field, watching children playing various games. They were greatly intrigued by the antics of one group, until it dawned upon them that the children were acting out something most adults love to watch—a wedding!

They watched the children's solemn efforts with much interest, and were specially intrigued by one little girl in a nurse's uniform who left the party to whisper something to another little girl who was sitting apart but really enjoying the scene. Unable to withhold her curiosity, one of the women leaned over the fence, and asked the little loner why she did not join the others in their game. "Oh, but I am in it," she smiled. "You see, I'm the baby—waiting to be born!"

SATURDAY—MAY 23.

THE Greek writer Aesop invented the form of short story with a meaning which we call a fable. One which I have always found amusing and meaningful tells of a boy who went bathing in a river and got out of his depth. He was about to sink when a traveller came by.

"Help! Help!" shouted the boy, but the traveller began to read the boy a lecture for his foolishness. The boy cried out, "*Save* me now and read me the lecture afterwards."

Good advice when others need or seek our help.

SUNDAY—MAY 24.

WHITHER thou goest, I will go; and where thou lodgest, I will lodge: thy people shall be my people, and thy God my God.

MONDAY—MAY 25.

I DO not know who Edward Tuck is or was, but he has left us this lovely little poem:

Age is a quality of mind.
If you've left your dreams behind,
If Hope is cold,
If you no longer look ahead,
If your ambition's fires are dead,
Then you are old.

But if from Life you take the best,
If in Life you keep the zest,
If Love you hold,
No matter how the years go by,
No matter how the birthdays fly,
You are not old.

TUESDAY—MAY 26.

WHEN the British runner Sebastian Coe broke the world record for the mile, he stopped being just well-known and became famous overnight. He was already holder of the world record for the 800 metres.

The newspaper reporters who flocked to interview him found Coe to be a dedicated and modest man. How did he feel about holding two world records at the same time, they wanted to know. "There is only one certainty," Coe told them. "The records aren't mine, they're only borrowed."

Well spoken, Mr Coe! What he said is true of much in our lives—our friends, relatives and all we have. They don't *belong* to us—they're only borrowed.

WEDNESDAY—MAY 27.

A GENTLE knock at the door, and there was little Jill, looking eagerly up at the Lady of the House.

"Would you like to hear a joke?" she asked.

"Come in and tell me about it," the Lady of the House said.

"Can you tell me," asked Jill, oh so seriously, "where is the best place to sharpen a pencil?"

She hardly waited for the Lady of the House to shake her head before she answered triumphantly: "The end, of course."

Jill asked two more riddles then dashed off to show her skill to Mrs Brown down the road.

A trivial incident? I don't think so, for when a little boy or girl accepts us two oldies as friends, do you know we feel as proud as if we'd been presented to the Queen?

THURSDAY—MAY 28.

OLD Bert had been a seafaring man for most of his days and had some great stories to tell about storms and hardships in far away places. His children listened to his tales, and so, in their turn, did his grandchildren. He was full of good advice, too, and in his rough way he steered them all, like a good pilot, through the sometimes choppy waters of family life.

"Cheer up," he used to say, when one of them came to him with a problem. "Worse things happen at sea before breakfast!"

With those words, bluffly spoken, he many a time put fresh fight into a faint heart. He knew that the more one worries over a difficulty, the larger and more terrible it appears. Tackle it quickly and as early as possible, and you can often amaze yourself with how easily and swiftly you find yourself in calm waters again.

FRIDAY—MAY 29.

THE following little poem was given to me by some friends who thought I might like to pass it on to readers. Not outstandingly good poetry, perhaps, but it was written by a man of their acquaintance who is blind. Here, then, is his simple expression of faith:

We who walk in darkness
And cannot see the light,
We know there's someone with us,
By day and by night.

Whether at work or play,
Or if we are on our own,
God is always by our side.
We never walk alone.

SATURDAY—MAY 30.

WHAT makes for success? Hard work, determination or just plain luck? All three seem to enter into it.

George Cadbury, of the famous chocolate firm, believed that integrity, a sense of purpose and a Quaker upbringing were behind his success. He made his dreams reality by unhesitatingly carrying out his schemes. And he knew how to draw the best out of others.

Poor health need be no deterrent to success. A classic example is R.L. Stevenson's continual fight against illness which did not prevent him from becoming a famous author. Schumann became a composer when one of his fingers became paralysed and he had to give up hope of becoming a famous pianist.

Demosthenes, a great orator, stammered hopelessly when he first spoke in public. With determination and grit he worked for three months to overcome his impediment. Disraeli, the great Victorian statesman, was howled down when he made his first speech in the House of Commons, but later, members hung on his words.

Sir Winston Churchill was not always a brilliant orator. As a young man he practised coining the telling phrases that later flowed from his lips and pen so readily. Churchill's motto was " Never run away from anything. NEVER!"

Perhaps that is the best advice of all.

SUNDAY—MAY 31.

BECAUSE he hath inclined his ear unto me, therefore will I call upon him as long as I live.

YOUNG IN HEART

When we were lively little girls
In days we can't forget,
We couldn't wait on holidays
To get our toes all wet.
And now we're old—but young in heart—
We love to paddle yet.

JUNE

MONDAY—JUNE 1.

SINCE she was quite small, my niece Joanna has loved learning and reciting poetry. Here is the piece she recited when she came to tea last Sunday:

The nicest thing in all the world
Is just a cosy sort of friend
With whom I am so much at home
I talk and chatter without end;
And when at last I've finished all
The things I have to say
I know my chum will never give
My secret thoughts away;
And that is why I share with you
When I've an hour to spend,
Because I always find you such
A cosy sort of friend.

Joanna smiled when I praised her for speaking so clearly, then suddenly she looked serious.

" Uncle Francis, I wish you weren't my uncle, then you could be my friend," she said.

Wasn't that lovely? Although so young, Joanna has already learned what a precious thing friendship is.

TUESDAY—JUNE 2.

TWO elderly Dalesmen received personal invitation cards from their vicar to attend a special gathering. At the foot appeared the letters RSVP.

They were a bit puzzled as to what the letters meant, but eventually one of them arrived at a solution: " It must be ' Refreshments Supplied by the Vicar of the Parish ' !"

WEDNESDAY—JUNE 3.

IT'S amazing what you find out when you're weeding behind the garden hedge and all the children of the neighbourhood are playing on the other side. You learn what Mr Smith says to his wife when he comes home from work and gets a plate of cold soup, how often Mrs Brown goes to the hairdresser, why the Jacksons can't afford a holiday this year and that little Betty Brown loves her granny better than her Aunt Isobel.

There are no secrets when the children are playing, but this I have noticed: when they start bragging about their parents, the father and mother of every girl and boy are tops. Parents don't hear this talk as often as the man behind the hedge. Perhaps it's a pity. It would make them proud—and humble.

THURSDAY—JUNE 4.

A FEW years ago York Minster was in danger of falling down. During the extensive repairs the peace of the ancient building was inevitably shattered by the clamour and disruption of excavation and building.

One day, in the midst of it all, the sound of pneumatic drills was competing with the strains of the organ on which Dr Francis Jackson was rehearsing. Half-seriously the surveyor asked him, "What note is that drill playing, Dr Jackson?" Immediately, the reply came, "E Flat!" And that moment, Francis Jackson said later, was when his "Sonata on the Re-birth of a Cathedral" was born.

There is beauty all around us if we have eyes to see it, and ears to hear it—even in the sound of a pneumatic drill!

FRIDAY—JUNE 5.

ELSIE, a good friend of mine, seems to wear a perpetual smile. One day I complimented her on it and asked her how she did it.

She smiled at my question and said, " It's just a matter of sharing. When I see someone without a smile, I give them one of mine."

SATURDAY—JUNE 6.

FRANCES RIDLEY HAVERGAL, who died in June 1879, wrote many hymns that have stood the test of time and are still sung today. After she died her sister Maria wrote:

" We do not often see the risings of our rivers, the tiny spring lies hidden in some mountain home. Even when the stream gathers strength in its downward course, it meets with many an obstructing boulder, passes through many an unfrequented valley and traverses here and there a sunless ravine. But the river deepens and widens, and is most known, most navigable, just as it passes away for ever from our gaze, lost in the ocean depths.

" And thus it was with the early life of that dear sister whose course I would now attempt to trace . . . "

Writing to a friend, Frances herself once said:

" If I am to write to any good, a great deal of *living* must go to a very little *writing* . . . "—the same sentiments neatly expressed.

In this age of instant coffee, instant puddings and instant potato, we tend to want—and expect—" instant success " as well. It is good to be reminded that time has much to teach us and that all we seek may not be ours until our later years.

SUNDAY—JUNE 7.

A NEW commandment I give unto you, That you love one another.

MONDAY—JUNE 8.

AFTER Helen Keller, who became deaf and blind before she was two, had learnt to communicate, she was asked what things she would most like to see. A baby's face came high on her list, also the faces of her relatives and friends. She also indicated that she would love to watch children at play, to visit a park, and watch the sun rise.

With so many wonders to see in the world, isn't it significant that Helen Keller should have chosen such ordinary things? To me it is humbling that the most precious things to someone deprived of sight should be the very ones that we take most for granted.

TUESDAY—JUNE 9.

I READ in a medical journal recently that some broken bones knit together in such a way that they become stronger than they were before being fractured. That got me thinking, not about broken bones but about friendships, which are often broken by quarrels. Even when friendships are not broken we often have the feeling that they are spoiled by disagreements and will never be the same again. Well it's true that they will never be exactly the same, but broken or tarnished friendships can be mended *and* often become stronger as a result.

It begins with someone having the courage to say, " I'm sorry."

WEDNESDAY—JUNE 10.

HAVE you ever come across this remedy for a fit of the blues? The cure is simply to look only for the good things around us. The man who goes into his garden to look for caterpillars and weeds will no doubt find them; his neighbour, going out to look for flowers, will return to his house with an armful of blossoms.

THURSDAY—JUNE 11.

DURING my cousin Lorna's holiday in Devon she came, late one afternoon, to a thatched cottage tucked away between trees on a clifftop. TEAS said a faded notice and Lorna, hot and thirsty, walked hopefully up the garden path.

A little old lady welcomed her into a cool parlour and promptly put the kettle on. Soon Lorna was drinking a welcome cup of tea and eating a delicious slice of home-made cake. She chatted for an hour or so to the friendly old lady, who insisted on giving her the rest of the cake when she left. Lorna laughingly protested that her Teas would not pay if she gave almost-whole cakes away.

"It's too late for more customers and I'll be baking again tomorrow," the generous little soul replied, then she pointed to some framed words hanging on the wall. "I *know* that's true," she added, pressing the wrapped cake into my cousin's hands.

Lorna turned and read: "We make a living by what we get, but we make a life by what we give."—Winston Churchill.

"Such wisdom tucked away in a remote little cottage!" Lorna commented as she shared her experience with me.

CONTEST

Of course it's fun,
But all the same
There's a lot to learn
From a friendly game.

FRIDAY—JUNE 12.

HAVE you ever wished that you could write one song or poem by which you would always be remembered? Few of us achieve such an ambition, so maybe this is why I look upon those of the past who have succeeded, with special respect and admiration.

For me, Robert Ramsay, former minister of Hillhead Baptist Church in Glasgow, is immortalised by the truth and insight of something he once wrote. It was not a song or a poem, but just one sentence. Here it is:

"You need to be very quiet to hear the footfall of God's presence in your life, but often we live such noisy lives that we fail to hear it."

Now read it again—and then listen.

SATURDAY—JUNE 13.

AFTER many years of distinguished service to one of our great hospitals, a surgeon was retiring and a special gathering was held to mark the event. As part of the tribute to him a plaque was unveiled bearing, in relief, a replica of his hand.

Many speeches were made praising the surgeon's skill, and then it came his turn to reply. He noted how many references had been made in the tributes to "the skill of the surgeon's hand," but he pointed out that the hand itself was controlled by the mind, and then he added something like this: "But behind the dexterity of the hand and the alertness of the mind there has to be a gentle touch that comes from the heart, a real compassion for one's patients."

Hand, head and heart—and for all of us, as well as surgeons, the greatest of these is heart!

SUNDAY—JUNE 14.

THE price of wisdom is above rubies.

MONDAY—JUNE 15.

TIME is such a a precious thing,
It's more than wealth untold!
It's something that we cannot store
And nobody can hold.
Life goes by so speedily,
Before we scarce can taste it,
And time can never be regained—
So why do people waste it?

TUESDAY—JUNE 16.

HAVE you noticed how ' down ' you feel after a long-faced acquaintance has burdened you with all the latest gloom and doom? Contrast this with the person who greets you with a friendly smile and cheery word. You go on your way lighter of step and the chances are that you pass the smile on to someone else.

It is a sobering thought, but you and I influence everyone we meet for better or for worse. St. Paul put it in a nutshell when he wrote: " None of us lives to himself".

The story is told that the Scottish preacher and hymn writer, George Matheson, once had a poor, shabby woman in his congregation who lived in a slum basement. Her neighbours were astonished one day to find her moving to a sunny garret. In answer to their questions she replied: " Ye canna hear George Matheson preach, and live in a cellar."

Do you and I depress or uplift? Deflate or inspire?

WEDNESDAY—JUNE 17.

THE house in which widowed Mrs Davies had lived for fifty years was due for demolition, and the day she was to move a great sadness swept over her. The building held so many memories and she had never wanted to live anywhere else.

Her daughter had offered her a home and that evening Mrs Davies sat in her room and tried hard to feel at home. Suddenly there was a little tap at the door and her smallest grandson crept in to join her. As he looked at the ornaments and snapshots she had brought with her she found herself recounting tales of old friends and old times.

The boy listened happily until bed-time. " I'm glad you've come to live with us," he told her frankly when he kissed her goodnight. " You'll be able to tell me lots of interesting things."

Mrs Davies smiled as the boy left her. There was a job for her after all. And to her delight she realised that her memories hadn't been tied to the stones of her previous dwelling. She had brought them with her.

THURSDAY—JUNE 18.

THE famous opera singer Janet Baker has given pleasure to thousands with her beautiful voice. She is a great artiste and also a warm, caring person. She once said:

" My gift is God-given and it must be given back. We all have a gift to give and if we give it with some sense of holy obligation, everything clicks into place. I feel the same about every child who is born. Help children find out what their gifts are, and we'll have healthy and happy children and unique and valuable lives."

FRIDAY—JUNE 19.

MOST children seem to have an innate sense of fair play. Little Philip, aged two, was playing in the sand with a few other slightly older boys when four-year-old John piped up, " I'm not going to let Philip dig in my hole."

Immediately, five-year-old Robin said, " Then he can dig in mine "—and promptly handed Philip his spade.

Moments later, John relented: " Philip can dig in my hole too if he wants."

We older folk can often learn a thing or two from the young ones.

SATURDAY—JUNE 20.

AT the rear of a fine family home in Suffolk was a large orchard that was often the target for thieves. One summer's day, young Thomas was busy sketching there when a face appeared over the fence. He rapidly sketched the features of the face before chasing the intruder away.

When Thomas told of the incident and produced his sketch, the likeness was immediately recognised as that of a local " character ".

Thomas Gainsborough was to paint many other portraits and landscapes—but his sketch of the raider is now regarded as a prototype of the present day " identikit ".

Gainsborough turned his sketch into a finished picture with the title " Tom Peartree's Portrait ".

SUNDAY—JUNE 21.

THE heavens declare the glory of God; and the firmament sheweth his handiwork.

MONDAY—JUNE 22.

HOW'S your life? Would you, like Shakespeare's Macbeth, describe it as a brief candle?

George Bernard Shaw would have none of it. "Life is no brief candle to me," he said. "It is a sort of splendid torch that I have got hold of for the moment."

TUESDAY—JUNE 23.

IF someone told you they'd seen a blue elephant, would you believe him?

Not likely! But if five hundred told you the same thing . . . well, you'd have to admit it must be true. That, really, is what a certain minister in Scotland was trying to put across to the congregation at an Easter Service I heard about. He said that if only one person had seen Jesus after his resurrection, it's doubtful if anyone would have believed it. But the fact is, he was seen by 500. Surely they couldn't all be mistaken?

"It's like this," he said. "If I ate a daffodil in the vestry in front of the church officer, you'd only have his word for it, and you might think he was mistaken." Then the minister left the pulpit, went over to a vase of flowers, pulled out a daffodil—and to their amazement, and the delight of the children, began to eat it!

Bit by bit, it disappeared, petals, trumpet and stalk, until he'd finished the lot. "Now," he said, "at least five hundred have seen me eat a daffodil—it must be true, mustn't it?"

The minister said afterwards that daffodils don't taste very pleasant—but I am sure that no sermon he has preached has ever made a bigger impression, or planted its message more firmly.

WEDNESDAY—JUNE 24.

HAVE you ever hesitated about helping a good cause because you felt your contribution would be so small it was hardly worth giving?

For thirty years Mother Teresa and the sisters of her community have devoted their time to helping the poorest of the poor in Calcutta and other parts of India. Once, talking about her work, Mother Teresa said, "It's only a drop in the ocean—but the ocean wouldn't be the same without that drop."

THURSDAY—JUNE 25.

OVER a hundred years ago in Normandy a small boy tramped from village to village trying to sell hats for his parents, who kept a hat shop. His name was Aristide Boucicault.

Life was a struggle for Aristide so he went to Paris to seek his fortune. He soon found employment as a draper's salesman and met and married his charming Marguerite, who had been a poor goose girl. Aristide then applied for a job at a boutique called Bon Marché. After he joined the staff, the shop began to prosper and eventually he was able to buy it himself. Marguerite was always at his side to help and encourage him. Together they made the shop famous for quality and good service.

They were both exceedingly generous, never forgetting their own poor beginnings. Marguerite devoted herself to the welfare of their staff and erected homes where they could recuperate after illness, and before he died it was to their staff that Aristide passed on the Bon Marché store—the first department store in Europe and still one of the most celebrated in the world.

PARTNERS

Man can build the loveliest things,
Create a joy to see,
When he, with Nature, hand in hand
Works in harmony.

FRIDAY—JUNE 26.

A TEACHER was talking to his class about their ambitions. One boy told him, " My ambition is to be famous and I don't mind what for."

" If you want to be famous," his teacher replied, " you must work hard and learn from the example of men like William Wordsworth, Albert Einstein, Stanley Matthews and Thomas Green."

" Who's Thomas Green?" asked the boy.

" You've never heard of him?" enquired the teacher.

" No."

" Well that proves my point," said the teacher. " He was an idle loafer!"

SATURDAY—JUNE 27.

YEARS ago I copied into my notebook these words from a church magazine. They were attributed simply to " A sermon by a negro preacher ":

" If all the sleeping folk will waken up, and all the lukewarm people will fire up, and all the disgruntled folk will sweeten up, and all the discouraged folk will cheer up, and all the quarrelling folk will make up, and all the lazy folk will shake up, and all the gossiping folk will shut up, then we shall have a good church."

And by the same rule, of course—a good home; a good school, office or workshop; a good village, town or city; a good nation; a good world.

SUNDAY—JUNE 28.

OUT of the mouth of babes and sucklings hast thou ordained strength.

MONDAY—JUNE 29.

WHEN a difficult task is lying ahead,
And you're fearful of making a move—
There's only one thing to help you along,
Only one way to improve:
Take the first step—don't sit there inert,
For that is the part that is worst—
The rest will be easy, once you begin,
But the hardest of steps is the first!

TUESDAY—JUNE 30.

WHEN I was young my hero was a writer named Charles Hamilton. He wrote schoolboy fiction, using over twenty pen-names and the best know of them was Frank Richards. Under this name he created Greyfriars School and the fat schoolboy Billy Bunter.

Frank Richards lived at Kingsgate-on-Sea, in Kent, and a friend has told me how one day he telephoned him to say how much he had enjoyed the Billy Bunter stories.

When the great man answered the telephone my friend was overcome with awe and could only mumble a few words of appreciation. Charles Hamilton told him that he was in the middle of writing a story and he gave a brief synopsis of it.

When the conversation came to an end Mr Hamilton said, "Goodbye—and thank you for ringing."

"I could hardly believe it, Francis," said my friend. "He was thanking me and I had interrupted his work, too. I've never forgotten it."

A "Thank you" sincerely said is never just a polite expression—it can be a very powerful message indeed.

JULY

WEDNESDAY—JULY 1.

LITTLE George and his mother were out walking when they passed a shoe-repair shop.

"Look, Mummy," George said, "Jesus must be in there. It says: 'Heeling while you wait'!"

THURSDAY—JULY 2.

"AGE," she claimed at the fine old age of 90, "does not wither me." It was Alison Uttley speaking, as she planned a new addition to her famous Little Grey Rabbit series of books.

There is a lovely story told of her. The pupils at a certain infant school loved her tales so much that one day their teacher suggested that they should write to Mrs Uttley. She did not realise what a pleasure it would bring to the author.

Alison Uttley corresponded with these children for 15 years. She loved their letters, and always replied to them. The children wrote Little Grey Rabbit stories of their own, and she signed their book covers and sent them special prizes for their efforts.

This busy, elderly, affectionate little lady makes me think of a challenging sentence written by André Maurois, the French author: "Growing old is no more than a bad habit which a busy man has no time to form."

Alison Uttley did not fall into this bad habit! Little Grey Rabbit was created when she was 45, and his adventures went on in her youthful mind for as many more years. No, age did not wither her.

FRIDAY—JULY 3.

MY friend Rosa was smiling broadly when I met her in our local shop the other day. "I can't help laughing, Francis," she said. "It's Jane."

Jane is her teenage daughter and she is forever asking to borrow the family car. That morning, exasperated, Rosa said to her, "What do you think the Almighty gave you two legs for?"

To which Jane at once replied, "One for the brake and one for the accelerator!"

SATURDAY—JULY 4.

I DON'T know if you are like me, but when I sing a specially lovely hymn I always want to know something about the writer. One of my favourite hymns is: "What a Friend we have in Jesus" written by Joseph Scriven who died almost 100 years ago.

I imagined him to be a man upon whom the sun always shone, one who was surrounded by a loyal circle of valued friends—yet who regarded Jesus as his supreme Friend. How wrong I was about the unbroken sunshine! Joseph Scriven faced many troubles, setbacks and disappointments. On the eve of his marriage his fiancée was drowned as she brought her wedding dress home by boat. Broken-hearted, Joseph Scriven left his native Ireland and emigrated to Canada. There his second fiancée died of a serious illness.

Did sorrow and adversity make him withdraw from society in a welter of self-pity? No! He devoted the rest of his days to helping the physically handicapped and others worse off than himself. He lived out the words of his hymn: "We should never be discouraged; take it to the Lord in prayer."

SUNDAY—JULY 5.

THE Lord shall preserve thy going out, and thy coming in, from this time forth, and even for evermore.

MONDAY—JULY 6.

WHEN Cliff Richard, the ever-youthful singing star, was taking part in one of his most successful London stage-shows he was asked by a reporter, " What's your favourite 'thing' at the moment?" To everybody's surprise he replied by saying, " Sundays."

He then went on to explain that, after a hectic week on stage, Sunday was the one day when he could relax, look forward to his Sunday dinner, and above all enjoy worship in church and the friendliness of his Crusaders class and Youth Fellowship. " I can't believe that anybody living it up in the West End could possibly get the satisfaction I do from an ordinary quiet, routine Sunday—as a Christian."

Well said, Cliff Richard!

TUESDAY—JULY 7.

THE great 19th-century Danish thinker Kierkegaard wrote several books which had an important influence on the development of philosophy. They are deep difficult works, little read by ordinary folk. But in his journals Kierkegaard often wrote with great simplicity, as in the following entry for July 7th 1838:

> " God creates out of *nothing*. Wonderful, you say. Yes, to be sure. But he does what is still more wonderful: he makes saints out of sinners."

WEDNESDAY—JULY 8.

JUST before his 85th birthday the veteran writer J. B. Priestley was interviewed by a reporter at his home not far from Stratford-on-Avon. He admitted that he didn't enjoy old age, but then he added these words: " Still, there's a part of you that's always youthful—deep inside." That was no doubt the secret of his tremendous output of creative writing. However old we are, we can remain young at heart.

THURSDAY—JULY 9.

THE Sunday School class had been told to write about " Grannies ".

With remarkable insight, seven-year-old Timothy wrote: " Grannies are people who have grown old on the outside, but are still young inside."

Well, aren't they?

FRIDAY—JULY 10.

OUR doctor has the most superb bedside manner. When he visits a patient he comes into the bedroom with a beaming face, as though greeting a long-lost friend. No matter how ill the person in bed might feel, he or she is soon cheered by the doctor's presence. After a careful examination he writes his prescription, gives his advice, and leaves with words of assurance and encouragement which are at least as important as his medical skill.

The bedside manner of a good doctor is something we might well adopt ourselves. We all ought to behave towards others as though we really care—and not just at the bedside, either!

SATURDAY—JULY 11.

IF cares and woe surround you
And you're feeling somewhat blue;
Just listen to the birds sing,
Watch how the flowers peep through;
Their message? That tomorrow
Will brighter be for you.

SUNDAY—JULY 12.

THE righteous shall flourish like the palm-tree: he shall grow like a cedar in Lebanon.

MONDAY—JULY 13.

I AM sure that, like me, you love to walk in a garden, surrounded by beauty, colour and scent. Our gardens are also full of living legends for many flowers and plants have stories which tell of their origin. Here is one of my favourite legends of the garden.

When morning first broke on the earth everything was new—the beasts, birds, flowers, trees and all that lived.

Then the day came when God the Creator gave everything a name. Afterwards he asked them all their names to make sure they had remembered.

He was pleased that their memories were so good—until he came to a little blue flower.

"What is the name I have given you?" asked God.

"I forget," she confessed.

God looked at the little blue flower he had made and smiled. "Forget *me* not," he said.

And so these charming and modest little blue flowers received the name forget-me-nots.

THE CROSSING

If life is like a flowing stream
We cross from day to day,
We're sure to find some stepping-stones
To guide us on our way;
And if each helps the other one,
The crossing can be lots of fun.

TUESDAY—JULY 14.

NOEL SCOTT of Birmingham sent me this message in rhyme which he titles " Helping Hand."

If help is needed, don't delay;
It may be wanted right away;
So volunteer at once, don't wait . . .
Next day—next week—may be too late!

WEDNESDAY—JULY 15.

JEAN and John Wilson had never seen London. So when they were invited south from Northumberland for their grandson's wedding it was a double thrill. From their hotel window they looked out over the Thames and the Houses of Parliament, which till then they had seen only in pictures or on TV.

Their grandson, Andy, is a London policeman and there were many young policemen at the wedding! John and Jean were the only granny and grandpa and what a time they had!

Afterwards, just as John and Jean were thinking of bed after a wonderful day, the telephone rang. Would they put on their coats and come downstairs? Wondering what was happening they did as they were asked.

In the entrance hall two young bobbies were waiting. They said they had arranged with Andy to take John and Jean on a night tour of London to see the lights and so the two old folk sped off through the brightly-lit streets to see the sights, with the policemen.

" They were so kind," said Jean. " And if anybody ever says to me again that the young men of today have no consideration for old folk, I'll soon tell them different!"

THURSDAY—JULY 16.

HAS it ever struck you that the best labour-saving idea ever invented consists of just one word—tomorrow? What a lot of things we put off doing today, thinking they will be somehow easier to face tomorrow, or in a day or two! But it's not true, is it? The irksome job and duties will be just as unpleasant in the future as they are now. Far better to face up to them and get the job done. So, come along! Let's not put off until tomorrow the work we can do today.

FRIDAY—JULY 17.

MY friend Bruce was a welfare officer. One summer day he cut an armful of roses from his garden and took them to a deprived area. He gave some to a blind lady who smelt them eagerly. "Such a change from the smells round here!" she exclaimed.

Bruce's last visit was to what is called nowadays a problem family. The eldest girl was on two years' probation. She stared sullenly when Bruce offered her the very last one of his roses. Then, to his surprise, she snatched it and held it against her cheek. "No one's never given me a rose before," she said. "I've never seed one close up."

My friend was touched by the reverence with which the girl fingered his gift. "My heart went out to her," he told me, "and I thought how different her life might have been if, earlier on, someone else had cared enough to give her a rose."

Sometimes it takes so very little to bring joy and beauty into another's life—and it can make so much difference.

SATURDAY—JULY 18.

ALTHOUGH the many translations of the Bible say the same thing, the choice of words can make a passage more memorable or clear. For example my favourite translation of the famous passage about love in Paul's letter to the Christians at Corinth is that in Dr Moffatt's Bible:

" Love is very patient, very kind. Love knows no jealousy; love makes no parade, gives itself no airs, is never rude, never selfish, irritated, never resentful; love is never glad when others go wrong, love is gladdened by goodness, always slow to expose, always eager to believe the best, always hopeful, always patient."

SUNDAY—JULY 19.

FOR he shall give his angels charge over thee, to keep thee in all thy ways.

MONDAY—JULY 20.

A FEW years ago I read of an English actress who had the unusual ambition of becoming a successful bullfighter in Spain. Despite the surprise and shock of her friends and the disbelief of bull-fighting promoters, she eventually overcame all difficulties and achieved her ambition.

When her first appearance was over she was asked how she had summoned up enough courage. In answer, she said that although it had needed courage she did not have the sense of satisfaction which she had expected. " There are greater forms of courage," she commented. " For many people—the sick, the handicapped and the lonely, for example—simply getting from day to day takes far more bravery than I could muster."

TUESDAY—JULY 21.

A FRIEND of mine has this verse by Dean Farrar pinned above his desk.

I am only one,
But I am *one.*
I cannot do everything,
But I can do something.
What I can do
I ought to do,
And what I ought to do
By the grace of God I will *do.*

WEDNESDAY—JULY 22.

I WAS mourning the loss of an old school friend, Robert, when my niece Joanna came for the weekend. Usually I enjoy Joanna's lively chatter but on this occasion I felt withdrawn, shut in with my own memories of days long past when Robert and I fished and climbed trees together. In my preoccupation I cut my finger and Joanna, who intends to be a nurse when she grows up, bound it eagerly.

On the Sunday morning Joanna removed the bandage and said solemnly: "Your wound needs air now, Uncle Francis. It will heal faster that way."

As I followed Joanna's advice I realised that it also applied to the deeper hurts of life. Sorrow wounds our hearts and, at first, the loving care and sympathy of those around minister to our needs. But eventually our hurt must be exposed to the "open air" of everyday life. As time passes, the normality of daily routine completes the healing process.

I have a strong feeling that my little niece will make a splendid nurse one day!

THURSDAY—JULY 23.

I LIKE to meet older people who retain their faith in youth. One man who never prejudged youngsters as being incapable of something was William Morris, the 19th century father of modern design in many fields, from furniture to typography, from textiles to interior decoration. He used to make a point of taking on apprentices who showed no particular aptitude for the work they would be doing, because he believed that every man could be trained to be a craftsman and an artist. The success of his ventures proved him correct in this conviction, and his faith in the abilities of young people shone untarnished throughout his life.

FRIDAY—JULY 24.

MR WATSON. Come here! I want you!"

Famous words—the first ever to be spoken over the telephone, just invented by Alexander Graham Bell. He had spilt some acid on his clothes, and used his invention to call for his assistant from the basement.

Actually, Bell had not set out to produce a telephone at all, but was trying to devise a better kind of deaf-aid. Fortunately he stumbled on something which has benefited all of us, including those who are hard of hearing.

What on earth would we do—I sometimes wonder—without our telephones? Oh, I'm well aware that when the phone rings it can sometimes be an infernal nuisance. But then I think of the blessing it can be both in emergencies and in keeping distant friends in touch. We can count Alexander Graham Bell as one of the great benefactors of mankind.

SATURDAY—JULY 25.

IN his essay " Grace Before Meat " Charles Lamb wrote: " I own that I am disposed to say grace upon twenty other occasions in the course of the day besides my dinner. I want a form for setting out upon a pleasant walk, for a moonlight ramble, for a friendly meeting, or a solved problem. Why have we none for books—those spiritual repasts—a grace before Milton, a grace before Shakespeare?"

A bit much? Perhaps. But don't you often feel the desire to say thank you for all the good things you enjoy? I know I do.

SUNDAY—JULY 26.

HE only is my rock and my salvation: he is my defence; I shall not be moved.

MONDAY—JULY 27.

ON the wall of his library at Buckingham Palace, King George V had six treasured maxims:

Teach me to be obedient to the rules of the game;

Teach me to distinguish between sentiment and sentimentality, admiring the one and despising the other;

Teach me neither to proffer nor receive cheap praises;

If I am called upon to suffer let me be like a well-bred beast that goes away to suffer in silence;

Teach me to win, if I may; if I may not, then above all teach me to be a good loser;

Teach me neither to cry for the moon nor over spilt milk.

TUESDAY—JULY 28.

SIR THOMAS BEECHAM, one of the greatest conductors of all time, started life as a brilliant pianist. He was also a keen sportsman, and particularly fond of cricket.

One day he was fielding during a cricket match when he fell awkwardly as he dived for the ball. His right wrist was injured, and for a long time afterwards he had no feeling in his fingers, so that he was unable to play the piano.

"And that's why," he once said to an interviewer, "I decided to become a conductor."

Just another example of how a set-back can be transformed into a new and promising way forward.

WEDNESDAY—JULY 29.

LITTLE Rachel came home from school miserable because another girl had called her "Fatty".

"You're not a bit fat," said her mother, hugging her. "And you've got lovely little legs!" Rachel's face lit up with pleasure and she ran out to play.

A few hours later her mother overheard her chatting to the elderly lady next door. In the middle of the conversation she said confidentially, "My mummy said I've got lovely legs."

"And so you have, Rachel," her neighbour agreed. "They're a lot nicer than my old skinny ones, aren't they?"

There was a pause, then "Y-e-s," said Rachel uncertainly, and then, consolingly she added, "But yours have always got such lovely shoes on the end!"

QUIET HAUNTS

They leave such happy memories,
These picturesque retreats
Of cobbled lanes and latticed panes
Away from busy streets.

THURSDAY—JULY 30.

JUST wealth enough to give and spare,
Just health enough to banish care,
Just friends enough sincere and true,
What more want I?
What more want you?

FRIDAY—JULY 31.

HOW quickly quarrels can sometimes spring up, even between newly-weds!

Two young friends of ours shared this story with us. One morning, Susan left her housework to chase two small boys from the flower bed her husband Tim had just planted. The boys found the ball they were searching for and Susan returned to her housework.

Later she grumbled at Tim for bringing so much grass into her freshly cleaned hall. He had mown the lawn that morning but was certain he left his shoes outside so it could not have been him. Susan declared hotly that it couldn't possibly have been her since she hadn't been into the garden—and they had a silly quarrel about it.

It was evening before she remembered about the two boys looking for their ball.

"How reluctant I was to admit that I was in the wrong!" Susan told us with a wry smile. "But, at last, I swallowed my pride, owned up and said I was sorry. It was so lovely to make it up!"

As the great 19th century preacher C.H. Spurgeon once said:

A little explained,
A little endured,
A little forgiven,
And the quarrel is cured.

AUGUST

SATURDAY—AUGUST 1.

TODAY is Lammas Day, Loaf-mass Day. In Anglo-Saxon times a loaf made of the first flour ground from that year's harvest was offered to God. The idea came from the Old Testament with its rules about the offering of first fruit.

Lammas Song

If you wait till the harvest is gathered,
If you wait till the leaves all fall,
If you wait till the harvest is gathered,
You may never never give at all.

If you wait till you're rich before helping
You may wait till the leaves all fall.
If you wait till you're rich before helping
You may never never help at all.

SUNDAY—AUGUST 2.

REJOICE with me; for I have found my sheep which was lost.

MONDAY—AUGUST 3.

WHEN I was a child I kept an autograph book and asked aunts, uncles, teachers and friends to write in it. Some just signed their names or expressed their best wishes. Others were thoughtful enough to write down little bits of wisdom. They were for fun, but some of them I have never forgotten. For instance one uncle wrote for me:

"An ounce of pluck
Is worth a ton of luck."

Something worth remembering at any age.

TUESDAY—AUGUST 4.

I DON'T know who first asked this question, but I think it's a good one and I put it to you:

"Do you make things happen, watch things happen, or wonder what on earth has happened?"

WEDNESDAY—AUGUST 5.

THE sun was shining as I came up the path. I was looking forward to my meal and a chat. Then the Lady of the House came out to meet me. "Come on, Francis," she said. "It's such a lovely evening—let's take a walk round the garden before you come in." Well, I confess, my heart sank just a little. You see, for some reason I hadn't been keeping the garden as well as I should have, and it had been a bit on my mind.

As we progressed, I couldn't help noticing the odd dandelion in the grass, a patch or two of grass between the vegetables, not to mention weeds in the border. But Mrs G., bless her, didn't seem to notice any of these. She praised the tiny blooms on the miniature roses which are such a joy to me, admired the honeysuckle, and we stood together enjoying the scent of the pinks. Gradually it dawned on me that, in half-expecting a rebuke, no matter how cheerfully delivered, I was doing Mrs G. a wrong. She was seeing the flowers. It was I who had taken so long to see past the weeds.

That's why I went in telling myself that while conscience is a fine thing, we are only human. And it's as well to remember it. Too much conscience can spoil an otherwise harmless joy—that's the moral from my walk round the garden.

Or am I only making excuses for myself!

THURSDAY—AUGUST 6.

YOUNG Freddie, aged six, was just beginning to understand the value of money. One day he announced to his mother that he was going to sell his toy wooden garage. His mother tried to put him off by suggesting that he would only get about a pound for it—so why not keep it in the loft for when he had a little boy of his own?

Freddie thought for a moment, and then replied that he didn't like the idea. A little boy of his wouldn't give him more than a pound for it either!

FRIDAY—AUGUST 7.

FOR well over half a century Miss Jean Gall, in her pilgrim's bonnet, was a much-loved figure in the streets of Dundee. She played the organ at open-air services.

Later, she took over a hall and led a mission, and hundreds of the poor, the alcoholics and the homeless came to bless her name.

"Ma" Gall, as she came to be known, was blind from birth. Yet those who knew her were aware that she had a gift more valuable than sight. I have just been reading a tribute paid to her after her death by a man who remembered her at a Sunday School service.

He describes how, as she sang the words of one of the great Redemption hymns and came to the line, "I'll carry my sunshine with me wherever I go," her face shone with an inner radiance. He never forgot that moment. "When I am feeling a bit down," he wrote, "that message is wafted back through the years, the clouds lift and the sun breaks through." Only the truly great in spirit can leave such a memory.

PLEASURE

Young or old,
Man or boy,
There are some things
All ages enjoy.

SATURDAY—AUGUST 8.

CHARLES DICKENS may have had h
but there could not have been much
with a man who could say:

"Whatever I have tried to do in life, I h
tried with all my heart to do well; whatever I ha
devoted myself to, I have devoted myself to completely. In great aims and in small, I have always
been thoroughly in earnest."

SUNDAY—AUGUST 9.

IT is more blessed to give than to receive.

MONDAY—AUGUST 10.

ONE evening Martin Luther, the German Reformer, saw a small bird perched on a tree, settling down to roost for the night. Thought Luther: "This little bird has had its supper, and now it is getting ready to go to sleep, secure and content, not troubling itself what its food will be, or where its lodging tomorrow. Like David, it 'abides under the shadow of the Almighty.' It sits on its little twig content, and lets God take care."

In watching that bird, was not Luther following the advice that Jesus gave in the Sermon on the Mount?—"Do not be anxious about your life, what you shall eat or what you shall drink, nor about your body, what you shall put on . . . Look at the birds of the air: they neither sew nor reap nor gather into barns, and yet your Heavenly Father feeds them."

How much anxious fretting we would save ourselves if, like Martin Luther, we remembered to do as we were commanded—and lived a day at a time.

TUESDAY—AUGUST 11.

ONE of my teachers used to tell me, "If a thing's worth doing it's worth doing badly."

I used to think this rather foolish. Now I know that I shall never play the piano like a concert pianist, sing like a professional, or produce a garden to compare with the very best. Even so I shall continue to play, sing and garden because these are some of the things I enjoy. They harm no one and give me pleasure so they are worth doing to *my* very best even if that's doing them rather badly.

WEDNESDAY—AUGUST 12.

CHARLES WICKSTEED, a wealthy industrialist, bought a piece of land at Kettering, in Northamptonshire, and set about planning a fine park. Every day he and his little dog Jerry went along to see how the work was progressing. They watched it beginning to take shape with grassy slopes, trees and a large lake. A children's playground was laid out with swings and other equipment.

Then Mr Wicksteed had to go abroad. When he came back he learned that Jerry had been killed by a car.

Today if you visit Wicksteed Park you will see a little statue of Jerry in the rose gardens.

The inscription reads:

" Closely bound to a human heart,
Little brown dog, you had your part
In the levelling, building, staying of stream
In the Park that arose from your Master's dream."

The park is administered by a Trust and visited by thousands of people from all over Britain each year.

SANCTUARY

The world is changing far too fast,
Or so some folks will say,
But there are places still that lie
Unchanged from yesterday.
And there, away from strife, a man
Can ponder on the Master's plan.

THURSDAY—AUGUST 13.

MANY years ago the Danish sculptor Thorwaldsen returned home from Italy taking with him several of the works of art that had won him fame. He had worked long and hard in Rome, and he had completed several marble masterpieces.

In Denmark, his servants unpacked the statues, scattering the ground with the straw in which they were packed. The following summer, flowers from the gardens of Rome bloomed in Copenhagen, sprung from the seeds he had carried with him unawares.

So not only was the sculptor's skill immortalised in marble, but unwittingly he had brought back fragrance and gladness for all who passed his way.

This story set me thinking. Could it be that in the final reckoning it will not be the great achievements of our lives that will count most? Perhaps it will be the unconscious words and little deeds of kindness that will be remembered.

FRIDAY—AUGUST 14.

RACHEL, who spends her holidays as a nursing auxiliary, often tells me of some heart-warming experience from her hospital ward. She finds her geriatric patients particularly cheerful.

For example, she was talking to old Mr Johnson, settling him down for his night's rest. Rachel thought it would be best if she removed his dentures for the night. Mr Johnson let her take them, then commented with a toothless grin: "Ee! I bet I look a right old man without my teeth!"

Mr Johnson, by the way, is ninety-six!

SATURDAY—AUGUST 15.

RAIN can be annoying, I don't deny it, especially if you have been looking forward to a lovely day out-of-doors. When I feel tempted to grumble a bit about a rainy day I remind myself of the words of an old countryman I knew years ago. If he heard somebody criticising the wet weather he used to say, "Well, it's the Lord's garden—He can water it when He likes." And he would quietly get on with his work.

SUNDAY—AUGUST 16.

FOR in him we live, and move, and have our being.

MONDAY—AUGUST 17.

"A KISS from my mother made me a painter," said the 18th century American, Benjamin West.

What he meant was that his wise mother's approving love set her son's feet firmly on the road to success. But for the encouragement she gave when the young Benjamin showed her his first crude efforts, he would never have persevered.

How different that painter's life story might have been had his mother frowned at his childish endeavour or wounded his spirit by ridiculing his artistic attempts.

We adults are equally sensitive when it comes to disapproval or a disheartening sneer. Lack of appreciation has made many a man abandon what might have been a great career. Encouragement costs so little. We should never grudge giving it where it is deserved.

TUESDAY—AUGUST 18.

PERHAPS the most demanding of all the Olympic athletic events is the Decathlon which comprises the 100 metres, the long jump, putting the shot, high jump, 400 metres, 110 metre hurdles, discus, pole vault, javelin and 1500 metres.

William Toomey, who won the gold medal for this event in the 1968 Olympics, is quoted as saying, " In the Decathlon you don't need cheers, deadlines, or even anyone to watch you perform. It's like religion, or painting or poetry. There's enough satisfaction in just doing it."

WEDNESDAY—AUGUST 19.

UNLESS you have faith as a little child . . ." My friend Bruce, who was a Welfare Officer until he retired, told me that he used to wonder what Jesus meant by that.

For many years Bruce visited deprived families in the slums, where he won the love and confidence of many poor, ill-kempt children, for whom he always had a kind word. Andy, a pale, thin little lad who lived with his grandmother, particularly looked forward to a visit from Bruce.

One day Andy refused to say goodbye to Bruce and trotted beside him down several dark streets, past dingy tenements and through side alleys, until my friend became anxious for the little boy's safety.

" You must go back now or you'll be lost," he insisted.

" I'm not lost," Andy replied calmly. " I'm with you."

After that, Bruce never wondered again what He meant. Andy had shown him.

THURSDAY—AUGUST 20.

SOME farmers from the USA once visited the Yucatan in Mexico and saw sisal plants growing. Sisal, a vegetable fibre which is strong, flexible and durable, comes from the leaves of the plant. It is important to farmers as a raw material for twine, ropes, string and sacking.

The farmers were surprised to see so strong a fibre coming from a plant growing in the poor parched soil of Mexico. How much better it would grow in good soil! So they took some seeds home with them and planted them in the good rich soil of Florida.

As expected the seeds produced a bumper harvest, but to their horror the farmers discovered that no fibre had grown in the leaves. Tough fibres, they found, grow best where the conditions are hard and difficult.

You and I are like sisal fibre. A carefree easy life seldom brings out the best in our character; it's the difficulties of life that give us the chance to develop whatever strength of character we may possess.

FRIDAY—AUGUST 21.

THE evangelist D.L. Moody was once challenged by a complete stranger who said, " Let me tell you, Mr. Moody, that I don't like your methods."

" That's interesting," said Moody, " because I am not completely satisfied with them myself. Tell me, how do you win souls?"

" Oh . . . well . . ." hesitated the man in confusion. " I don't."

" In that case," replied the evangelist quietly, " I prefer the way I do it to the way you *don't*."

GOOD SERVANT

Happy the man who walks in the way
Of his Lord and Master day by day.

SATURDAY—AUGUST 22.

LIFE is like a garden
In many little ways.
Contentment cannot flourish
If gloom is all you raise.
Plant the seed of kindness
Wherever you may go,
Then, fertilised by commonsense,
Friendship's bound to grow.

SUNDAY—AUGUST 23.

ALL things work together for good to them that love God.

MONDAY—AUGUST 24.

ONE of the most popular radio programmes ever was " The Brains Trust," which started during the war, in 1941, and ran for many years. People sent in questions on every imaginable subject and a panel of experts did their best to answer them. They were asked about the origin of the universe, how flies walk on ceilings, why snakes are fascinated by music, why we can't tickle ourselves and make ourselves laugh, and thousands more questions.

One listener asked Professor C. E. M. Joad, " What is happiness?" Here is part of his answer.

" It is like a flower that surprises you; a song that you hear as you pass the hedge, rising suddenly and unexpectedly into the night. I would like to sum up by saying that the best recipe for happiness that I know is not having leisure enough to wonder whether you are being miserable or not. In other words happiness is a by-product of activity."

TUESDAY—AUGUST 25.

MRS CHRISTINE WOOD of Surbiton, Surrey, shared a moving incident with me which occurred shortly after the death of her husband at the early age of thirty-nine. A close friend called to apologise for, as he put it, letting her down in her hour of need. His failure? He had been unable to pray when he heard of Geoffrey's death. He had wept, but not prayed.

While he was apologising, a verse from Psalm 56 flashed into Mrs Wood's mind.

"Thou hast kept account of my tossings; put thou my tears in thy bottle! Are they not in thy book?"

"I was certain that our friend had prayed as earnestly as anyone," Christine wrote to me. "I told him so and he went away greatly cheered."

She says that she, too, was helped and that psalm has had a special meaning for her ever since. She now knows that we do not necessarily need words to pray. She doubts if God ever wants long speeches from us! Instead He hears every heartfelt sigh and our tears are among His best remembered things.

WEDNESDAY—AUGUST 26.

HERE are three little thoughts about getting on with our neighbours which I came across recently. I don't know who first said or wrote them, but I think you'll agree they are all very true:

A sharp tongue is the only tool that grows keener with constant use.

Faults are thick where love is thin.

Nothing so needs reforming as other people's habits.

FOR ALL AGES

It's fun for the children
To ride in the train,
Hear the hissing and snorting
Of steam once again.

Not only the children—
There's always a part
For grannies and granpas
Still young at heart.

THURSDAY—AUGUST 27.

MILLIONS of cinema-goers throughout the world have laughed heartily at the amusing antics on the screen of the popular American comedian Jerry Lewis. Behind his comical facial expressions and crazy ways is a first-rate actor who takes immense care with every detail in his performances.

Yet for some years now he has lived in constant physical pain which almost wrecked his film career. It all began in 1965 when he was appearing in cabaret at Las Vegas. During a performance he fell heavily which resulted in severe spinal injury. Hospital treatment gave him temporary relief, but as time went by Lewis was obliged more and more to resort to pain-killing drugs. Unhappy and depressed and in agony he decided one morning to kill himself. He pressed a loaded pistol to his mouth and was about to pull the trigger when suddenly he heard the sound of children's laughter nearby. He said afterwards, " The children's happy laughter snapped me out of committing suicide."

The ordinary things of everyday life can be a source of inspiration to us all: a new dawn; a walk in the hills; the first spring flowers; the sound of music floating across the street; even a simple friendly greeting. There's magic everywhere.

FRIDAY—AUGUST 28.

MANY proverbs are the same in most languages, but occasionally I come across one which doesn't really have an equivalent in English. I like this old saying from France: " One 'Here you are!' is worth more than two 'I'll let you have it soon!' "

SATURDAY—AUGUST 29.

OUR house is so much brighter, when you come here to stay,
Our troubles seem much lighter, and sad thoughts fly away;
We're sorry when you leave us, we hoped you would remain,
Now we're longing for the next time you visit us again.

SUNDAY—AUGUST 30.

REJOICE with them that do rejoice, and weep with them that weep.

MONDAY—AUGUST 31.

ONE of the most inspiring stories of patience and courage is that of Alexander Mackenzie's exploration of Canada. Born at Stornoway in the Hebrides he joined a group of fur-traders based on Montreal. On the 3rd June, 1789 he set out with thirteen companions in three canoes, determined to find a way through the unexplored north to the Pacific Ocean.

After 102 days and a hard journey of nearly 3,000 miles, Mackenzie reached an ocean—but, to his great disappointment, it was the Arctic, not the Pacific. Still, less than three years later he set out again, striking westwards through the Rocky Mountains. After struggling down dangerous rapids and dealing with several parties of hostile Red Indians he eventually reached the Pacific coast and saw what is now Vancouver Island.

When I think of the determination and endurance of explorers like Mackenzie, the little problems I meet on life's journey don't seem quite so daunting—and, like him, I press on!

PATIENCE

To shape a lovely tree you need
A seed, some rain, some sun,
A pair of shears—and fifty years—
And then you've just begun!

SEPTEMBER

TUESDAY—SEPTEMBER 1.

OH, we're not a bit old-fashioned," said the bride, laughing. Indeed they weren't! It was a very trendy wedding, to say the least. The bride was dressed in matching cream, lace trousers and jacket, and her groom looked incredibly dazzling in satin, blue dungarees. She'd had her hair dyed in a rather pretty soft shade of pink, and he wore a hooped ear-ring in one ear.

But I couldn't help noticing as she linked her hand in his, that she was rather proud of the plain gold band on the wedding finger of her left hand. Some traditions die hard and, between you and me, I'm rather glad about that.

WEDNESDAY—SEPTEMBER 2.

IN West Yorkshire, between Bradford and Halifax, there is a little woodland beauty spot known as "Judy Brig". The bridge was named after Judy North, a lively character who presided over some nearby tea-gardens about a century ago. One day Judy caught a local vicar digging up a small plant from her garden and she insisted on him paying for it. The vicar said he would take it home and see how it got on in his own garden. "I must first see if it thrives," he said. "Then I'll pay for it."

Some time later Judy took a baby boy to the vicar to be baptised. When the ceremony was over the vicar asked for the usual fee.

"Nay," said Judy, "I must first take him home to see if he thrives—then you'll have your fee!"

THURSDAY—SEPTEMBER 3.

I WAS chatting the other day to an aunt of mine who, before she retired, worked for a famous wedding-dress designer. She told me some of the little secrets of the workroom. Apparently, when a wedding dress was being put together, it was the custom for one of the team of seamstresses to pluck a hair from her head and sew it into the hem of the bridal gown for good luck.

I wonder how many happy, young brides know about this old custom? It's quite a charming one, isn't it?

FRIDAY—SEPTEMBER 4.

IT is said that Sir Walter Scott was considered by his teachers to be a dull pupil. Many times he was humiliated by having to stand in a corner wearing a dunce's cap.

The story is told that when he was twelve, he and his parents were invited to a house where the poet Robert Burns was staying. Burns admired a picture with a verse written under it, which hung on the wall. He asked who the author was but no one could tell—until Walter shyly stepped forward and spoke up. Not only did he name the author, but he also quoted the rest of the poem. Burns patted him on the head and said, "Ah, bairnie, ye will be a great man in Scotland some day."

It is said that Walter was so encouraged by those words that they started his feet on the road to success. The literary world might have been a much poorer place if that one sentence had remained unspoken.

We cannot all be great poets or writers, but we can be among the world's encouragers.

SATURDAY—SEPTEMBER 5.

"ONE Sunday, when I was out for a walk with my father . . ."

The congregation of Kirriemuir Old Parish Church, in the famous little town where Sir James Barrie was born, often hear their minister, the Rev. John Skinner, include in his sermon a wee story beginning with these words.

The other Sunday, I am told, Mr Skinner was talking about friendliness. Like most people who live in a village or small town, his father would give a greeting to everyone he met. One day father and son met a man the little boy was sure he had never seen before. However, just as he had done a dozen times already during their walk, his father nodded to the stranger and made a remark about the weather.

After they had passed on, the little boy asked his father, "Do you know that man?"

"No," said his father. "But if you don't speak to people you never get to know them."

If you and I find there are a lot of people round about us whom we don't know, perhaps we should remind ourselves of the good advice of John Skinner's father.

SUNDAY—SEPTEMBER 6.

I DO set my bow in the cloud, and it shall be for a token of a covenant between me and the earth.

MONDAY—SEPTEMBER 7.

ANOTHER day, another chance
To have a change of heart.
Throw off the yoke of yesterday
And make a brand new start!

TUESDAY—SEPTEMBER 8.

WHEN I hear people talk today about doing their own thing, I think of the famous piano accompanist, Gerald Moore. When asked why he hadn't chosen the more glamorous career of solo pianist he replied that the world was full of brilliant soloists, but really hard up for good accompanists.

We all need to practise working in harmony with others—not just in music but in everything we do.

WEDNESDAY—SEPTEMBER 9.

WHEN my niece Joanna was about three years old she usually enjoyed a cuddle, but one evening she showed no interest in climbing on to her mother's lap.

"It's time for your bedtime hug," her mother said, but Joanna went on playing with her bricks.

"Don't you want a cuddle?" her mother persisted.

Joanna sat back on her heels, looked at the brick tower she was building, then slowly turned her head to look at her mother. The next minute she ran to her, with her favourite teddy-bear in her arms.

"Here you are, Mummy. You can hug teddy, 'cos I'm busy," she said, and went straight back to her bricks.

We smile at these homely incidents, don't we, yet how often do we try to put people off with things? Books and bunches of flowers are very welcome to lonely shut-ins, but often it is our company that they crave. They long for us to give, not just things, but something of ourselves by staying a while for a friendly chat.

THURSDAY—SEPTEMBER 10.

THE poet Edgar A. Guest died some years ago, but his verses live on. " My Creed ", for instance has a lovely message for today:

To live as gently as I can;
To be, no matter where, a man;
To take what comes of good or ill
And cling to faith and honour still;
To do my best, and let that stand
The record of my brain and hand;
And then, should failure come to me,
Still work and hope for victory.

FRIDAY—SEPTEMBER 11.

DURING the 1939-45 War, Ludwig Guttman fled from Hitler's Germany and found refuge in Britain. He did more than that. He founded the National Spinal Injuries Centre at Stoke Mandeville, and as a result of his research into the conditions which cause paralysis, most of the patients at Stoke Mandeville are able to return home and resume normal employment.

In 1948, when London staged the Olympic Games, he initiated a special Olympiad of his own—the Paraplegic Olympic Games, in a successful attempt to imbue the disabled with a spirit of true sportsmanship which would encourage and inspire thousands of paralysed people.

In his own words, " No greater contribution can be made to society by the paralysed than to help, through the medium of sport, to further friendship and understanding amongst nations."

Thanks to the fine work of Sir Ludwig Guttman, the lives of countless people have been broadened and enriched.

SATURDAY—SEPTEMBER 12.

I KNOW the ladies won't mind if I tell a little joke against them. It's about the man whose wife gave him two ties for his birthday, a red one and a blue one. When he was getting dressed he decided to put on the red one.

When he came downstairs for breakfast his wife stared at him. " Ah," she said. " So you don't like the blue tie I bought you!"

SUNDAY—SEPTEMBER 13.

THE Lord is my shepherd; I shall not want.

MONDAY—SEPTEMBER 14.

SOME time ago I read a newspaper article by a gifted young writer called Judy Froshaug. She was born with what she calls a minor disability—she has no left hand. Tying her shoes, cutting up her own food, and serving at tennis are all obstacles that she has proudly overcome with skill and determination.

A doctor once suggested to her mother that she should try an artificial hand. She laughs now as she tells of how it dropped off in public. The man who was to be her husband picked it up, bowed and said with an engaging smile, " Madame, your glove, I believe!"

Now a mother, Judy has obviously come to terms with life. In her writings she gives a helping hand to others with disabilities—" warts " as she calls them.

God expects us all to make something worthwhile of our lives " warts and all." People like Judy, who start at an enormous disadvantage, show us how it can be done.

TUESDAY—SEPTEMBER 15.

BEFORE the American President Gerald Ford and his wife were married, they pledged that neither of them would try to change the other. Mrs. Ford claims that the guiding principle in their marriage has been the same as St. Francis of Assisi expressed in one of his prayers:

"Grant that I may not so much seek to be consoled as to console, to be understood as to understand, to be loved as to love; for it is in giving that we receive, it is in pardoning that we are pardoned."

It sounds a good recipe for a successful life, as well as for a happy marriage, doesn't it?

WEDNESDAY—SEPTEMBER 16

I DISLIKE Saturday shopping but helped the Lady of the House because we were expecting visitors. It was a windy day and an elderly lady cycled past with wisps of grey hair flying. An extra strong gust caught her unawares and she fell off her bicycle, scattering shopping.

We hurried forward to help but two small children beat us. The little girl helped the elderly rider to her feet while the boy gathered scattered vegetables. The undaunted old lady repacked her load and the girl held the bicycle until she remounted. She was only a little girl, but had just enough strength to hold the handlebars steady in spite of a heavy basket and the strong wind.

"What an example those children were," the Lady of the House remarked as we walked on. "So often we don't help people because we think we haven't enough to give, yet sometimes it takes very little to get another person going again."

It's worth remembering.

THURSDAY—SEPTEMBER 17.

A FRIEND of mine who teaches in a village primary school told me that though she had read hundreds of stories written by her pupils over the years, one of the most charming was the shortest. It read: " Every morning the sun comes up to see how we are all getting on. To his joy he finds that we are all lit up. In the evening he goes away feeling happy. He think we're always like that."

Isn't it a lovely thought?

FRIDAY—SEPTEMBER 18.

WHEN things trouble us in life, it's often good to take a walk in the countryside. The peace and beauty around help make us glad to be alive, despite life's worries. These thoughts were expressed long ago in these lines by an anonymous poet:

The little cares that fretted me
I lost them yesterday,
Among the fields above the sea
Among the lambs at play,
Among the lowing of the herds,
The rustling of the trees,
Among the singing of the birds,
The humming of the bees.

The foolish fears of what might happen,
I cast them all away
Among the clover-scented grass,
Among the new-mown hay,
Among the husking of the corn
Where drowsy poppies nod,
Where ill thoughts die and good are born—
Out in the fields with God.

SATURDAY—SEPTEMBER 19.

EVERY autumn, outside the Albert Hall in London, the queue gathers for the last night of the Promenade concerts. All sorts of people—many of them young and high-spirited—make the steps of the Albert Hall their home for two weeks to be sure of a good place at this very special concert.

Some take a fortnight's holiday while others go off to work every morning from the queue. Meals are cooked on camp stoves and contributions to the night's entertainment inside the hall are eagerly planned.

In his book "Here is the News," Richard Baker, the newscaster, tells us that he understands this enthusiasm—he queued the hard way for concerts in his own young days. "Now I don't have to queue," he says, "and when I slip through the stage door, I wonder if I'm not missing some of the excitement of it all."

Life without a challenge is a poor thing. It's the pleasures and prizes that we have worked and striven for that give us true delight.

SUNDAY—SEPTEMBER 20.

WEEPING may endure for a night, but joy cometh in the morning.

MONDAY—SEPTEMBER 21.

EIGHT-YEAR-OLD Peter was at the christening ceremony for his new baby brother. Afterwards the vicar jokingly asked Peter if he could take the new baby home with him.

"Oh, no," replied Peter, shocked. "*We* bought him—*you* only get to wash him!"

TUESDAY—SEPTEMBER 22.

SOME of the best stories are those with an unexpected ending. Like the story of the princess who made friends with a frog. One day the frog saved her from a fearful disaster. She bent to kiss him in gratitude.

"Stop!" said the frog. "I know what's going to happen. You're going to kiss me and I'll turn into a handsome prince. Then I'll have to live in a palace and meet lots of important people."

"Why yes, frog, dear," said the princess.

"No thanks," said the frog. "I like being a frog. In fact I enjoy it!"

So the frog went on being a frog. He'd acquired one of life's greatest gifts—contentment.

WEDNESDAY—SEPTEMBER 23.

WHEN winter is over and everything comes to life again, people get the urge to be on the move and to travel to new places.

Five hundred years ago, Geoffrey Chaucer wrote about this, so we haven't changed much. In Chaucer's day the journey was usually a religious pilgrimage. The most important was the pilgrimage to the shrine of Thomas à Becket at Canterbury, about which Chaucer wrote in his "Canterbury Tales."

Since the party travelled together they were obliged to travel at the pace of the slowest. This gave them time for music-making and story-telling. For many, the journey was fun and often better remembered than the purpose of the journey itself—arrival at the shrine.

Our lives are like that. Whatever we do, it is along the way that we shall find happiness and not at the end of the road.

THURSDAY—SEPTEMBER 24.

HAVE you got the correct time? It's surprising how frequently we allow clocks and watches to go fast or slow, so that we are constantly having to make a time-check. Did you know that there used to be a custom in Malta whereby there were always two faces on clocks in church—one showing the correct time, and one showing a false time in order to confuse the Devil about the time of the service?

I'm afraid we can fool neither the Devil nor ourselves by pretending about time. It moves on relentlessly, and it is up to us to make the most of every precious hour. With Kipling we must learn "to give the unforgiving minute sixty seconds' worth of distance run."

FRIDAY—SEPTEMBER 25.

RECENTLY the Lady of the House and I visited Bessie Firth, a faithful attender of our local church until advanced years and arthritis kept her at home. She was delighted to see us and made us most welcome.

When we were about to leave, this dear old lady went out to pick the choicest roses in her tiny garden for us to take home, and before handing them over to us she insisted on cutting off all the thorns.

Later, as the Lady of the House arranged the roses in our best vase, she remarked on how kind it was of old Mrs. Firth to cut off the thorns.

"It's the little things like that," she said, "that make life easier for other people."

She was right, of course. The small pinpricks of life can cause a lot of pain. It's up to all of us to cut off the thorns for other people.

DAY OUT

Reflected in the silent water
Patient anglers bide their time.
Ripples widen on the surface—
Flash of silver on the line.
Then homeward 'neath the setting sun,
Another day of fishing done.

SATURDAY—SEPTEMBER 26.

A HAMPSHIRE man of 89 was asked his recipe for a long, healthy, and happy life.

He gave a slow smile. " My formula lies in two simple words: ' Yes, dear.' "

SUNDAY—SEPTEMBER 27.

GOD so loved the world, that he gave his only begotten Son, that whosoever believeth in him should not perish, but have everlasting life.

MONDAY—SEPTEMBER 28.

IF you know about Bilbo Baggins you will have read *The Hobbit,* the fairy tale for children and adults by Professor J.R.R. Tolkien. Perhaps but for a mother's love and selfless devotion it might never have been written.

In Victorian times the family firm of Tolkien in Birmingham made pianos. Unfortunately the firm went bankrupt and Arthur Tolkien and his wife went to South Africa where two little boys were born—John and Hilary.

When Arthur Tolkien died, Mrs. Tolkien decided to return to England and settled at Sarehole, Birmingham, where she taught her two young sons at home. She saw that John was artistic and she spared no effort to encourage him with his paintings and drawings. She was the first to stir in him an interest in ancient languages which influenced the whole course of his life and led to his brilliant academic career.

The mother of Professor J.R.R. Tolkien not only encouraged her children but imprinted upon them strong and durable standards. She has left a legacy for the world to share.

TUESDAY—SEPTEMBER 29.

WE were cycling along a lonely country road, the Lady of the House and myself, when she suddenly said, " Ring your bell. That's Mary Hodge's cottage."

I duly obliged and as I did so I looked across the little garden, with its old-fashioned flowers, to Mary Hodge's front door.

" Nobody there," I said. " She won't know who it is."

" That doesn't matter," said the Lady of the House. " You know what Mary told us: ' Every time you pass and ring your bell, I'll know you're thinking of me '."

What a happy idea! And how many lonely people would welcome just a little sign of some sort that somebody is thinking of them!

WEDNESDAY—SEPTEMBER 30.

SHE is a widow who lives alone, but as we did not know her very well we almost didn't bother to send Mrs Mitchell a card when we were on holiday. But—just as an afterthought really—we added her name to the end of our list, and sent her a view of the seaside.

" Thank you so much for the lovely card," she smiled when we happened to meet in the street some weeks later. " It really helped me to know someone was thinking about me that day."

She told us that by the same post she'd had a card from the hospital giving her the date to go in for an operation. This rather depressed her, but our card cheered her up again at just the right moment.

Just shows where an afterthought can lead, doesn't it?

OCTOBER

THURSDAY—OCTOBER 1.

I KNOW a lot of folk who are very fond of liquorice all-sorts. Did you know that they owe their existence to an accident? One day in 1890 a salesman called Charlie Thompson was delivering a great pile of different bags of liquorice sweets, when the whole lot slipped from his grasp and ended up a jumble on the floor. The mixture of several different types and colours of sweets looked so attractive that it was decided to sell them like that in future. The new assortment soon caught on and has remained one of the most popular lines ever since.

Not all accidents are unfortunate, are they? If we have a slip-up today, let's see if we can learn something from it, and turn it to our advantage.

FRIDAY—OCTOBER 2.

IF you've heard this story before, no matter. The point it makes is always worth repeating. Two young brothers were asked by their mother to take some food to an old lady. She asked them each to choose a basket. One filled a large basket, but his brother managed to find a small one, so that he would have less to carry.

The old lady was so delighted to receive the food that she made the boys a present of apples from the tree in her garden. They could have as many as they could carry away. That's right, the boy who had selfishly chosen the small basket carried home far fewer apples than his more willing brother. Just a story, but it's still true that the more we give, the more we receive.

SATURDAY—OCTOBER 3.

THERE is a lonely inn on the Yorkshire moors between Pickering and the coast which is visited by tourists from all over the world. They come to the old Saltergate coaching inn, not because of any famous person connected with it—but because of its peat fire. You see, it has been kept burning continuously ever since 1801, and the present inn-keepers, Paul and Christine Coverdale, have no intention of letting it go out.

There's nothing nicer than a cosy fire, and I find something quite inspiring in the idea of one which burns on through the centuries. As a symbol of hospitality, how important it is to "keep the home fires burning."

SUNDAY—OCTOBER 4.

THE earth is the Lord's, and the fulness thereof; the world, and they that dwell therein.

MONDAY—OCTOBER 5.

HARVEST time reminds us that we are not self-sufficient creatures but are dependent on one another, and ultimately on forces beyond our control for "life and breath and all things."

We often forget this, as did the small boy who is reputed to have said, "We don't need to say grace in our house; my mum's a good cook!" But our daily bread comes not just from Mum or from the shop round the corner. The harvest hymn reminds us,

Back of the loaf is the snowy flour
And back of the flour is the mill
And back of the mill is the wheat and the shower,
And the sun and the Father's Will.

TUESDAY—OCTOBER 6.

WHEN the singer Mario Lanza died in 1951, some newspapers accused him of conceit, bad temper and other faults. They chose to seize on anything that might show the bad side of his character and they completely overlooked his fine qualities of generosity and humour, his politeness to his thousands of fans and his love of family life.

Luckily, in time, good is always more powerful than bad. Today Mario is remembered with affection throughout the world. Here in Britain I am told there is a flourishing Mario Lanza Society where members meet together not just to listen to his voice on records and to watch his films, but often simply to recall the kind of person he was. They choose to remember only the best of Lanza—and why not?

WEDNESDAY—OCTOBER 7.

PERFUMES are made from the oil of flowers. I knew that much, but it wasn't until recently that I read that this special oil is found in different parts of various plants. In jasmine and the rose it is found in the petals; in the violet it is in both the flowers and the leaves. In lavender it is found only in newly-opened flowers.

Some aromatic plants have only to be touched to release their pent-up fragrance. Think of the sweet-scented leaves of certain geraniums, or the delicate lemon-scented thyme. Then there are the many varieties of sages and mints.

Can it be that we, as people, can make life sweeter for others in some way? For some of us our special fragrance will take the form of kind actions or a few helpful words. Or we might need only to say a quiet, simple prayer for a friend.

THURSDAY—OCTOBER 8.

DID you ever know a child to be lost for an answer? A lady I know did some baby-sitting for friends who had a particularly lively child. He kept getting out of bed and she kept sending him back.

Eventually she lost patience and shouted, "Whatever are you doing out of bed now?"

"It's alright," he said meekly. "I'm just tucking myself in."

FRIDAY—OCTOBER 9.

I ONCE heard a preacher suggest that we should compare the troubles we have in the course of a year with a large bundle of sticks that are too large for us to lift. Fortunately we do not have to carry them all at once. God unties the bundle, he said, and allows us to carry one stick each day. This we could easily do—if we met our troubles one at a time. But, the preacher continued, many of us choose to carry yesterday's stick again today and often add tomorrow's stick before we need to carry it. If only we would meet our troubles one at a time, he said, what a lot of unnecessary anxiety we would save ourselves.

SATURDAY—OCTOBER 10.

SAYS Mrs Thomson, when I leave,
"We've had a lovely crack,
I hope it won't be long until
I see you coming back."
I smile and thank her, for I know
Although my words don't glisten,
I give the poor soul all she needs—
Someone to sit and listen.

SUNDAY—OCTOBER 11.

AND now abideth faith, hope, charity, these three: but the greatest of these is charity.

MONDAY—OCTOBER 12.

BILL and Jane decided to give their small son Neil a treat. They took him to a seaside resort where the R.A.F. aerobatic team, the Red Arrows, were giving a display. A thrilling show it was, too, and Bill and Jane stood on the beach staring upwards, spellbound.

Three-year-old Neil, however, was not impressed. He hardly glanced at the planes—he was too busy playing with the sand and pebbles at his feet.

Children often teach us the valuable lesson that there is joy to be found in the simple things of life.

TUESDAY—OCTOBER 13.

ONE of the most beautiful words in the English language is "home". What a depth of meaning it conveys! I heard a story recently about a man who was watching his neighbours and their children being evicted from their home. As their belongings were loaded into a lorry to be moved to temporary accommodation he noticed that the family looked strangely unconcerned at their plight.

He went across to them as they stood by the lorry. "You poor things," he said. "How awful it must be to have no home."

The youngest child looked up at him. "But we do have a home," he said. "It's just that we have nowhere to put it."

WEDNESDAY—OCTOBER 14.

FIVE-YEAR-OLD Jimmy was charmed when he learned that the lovely cosy jersey Gran was knitting was for him. Two or three times a day he came up to her to inspect progress. However, Gran was at Jimmy's home for just a week's holiday and half way through the week he was clearly becoming anxious about the work rate.

"Gran," he asked. "Are you doing that jersey bit by bit?"

"Yes, Jimmy," answered Gran seriously. "Bit by bit. It's the only way I know."

I am glad to report that shortly after her return home Gran got the jersey finished and Jimmy is now the proud wearer. I have to add that in his family that jersey will always be known as "Jimmy's bit-by-bit jersey". Not the blue and grey or the Shetland-knit, but just the "bit-by-bit"!

THURSDAY—OCTOBER 15.

I CALLED to give my condolences to an old friend whose husband had just died. Seven or eight members of her family were present and as we talked about "Dad" and how much he had meant to us all, I noticed that his widow had quietly slipped out. I thought that perhaps she was finding it all too much for her, but shortly she returned, perfectly composed. Then, as I was leaving, I noticed a large bunch of roses on the hall table. My friend gave them to me. "I just went out to pick these in the garden," she said. "Will you take them to your wife with my love?"

Amid her own grief she had still found room to think of others. Can you wonder that I raise my hat today to her courage and faith?

FRIDAY—OCTOBER 16.

A WISE old monk was walking round the monastery gardens with a very young and nervous novice, teaching him to meditate and pray in complete silence. As they were walking in the clear morning light the novice was moved to whisper, "Isn't the peace here wonderful?"

Later that night, when they had finished the last service of the day, the old monk whispered back to him, "It is—but don't spoil it again by talking!"

A peace which is broken needlessly, becomes *a piece.*

SATURDAY—OCTOBER 17.

ALL her life Mrs Mary Williams had been comfortably off and she had given generously to many charities. Then misfortune struck and she found herself in straitened circumstances.It was a great blow to her pride. Many a helping hand was offered, but Mrs Williams stubbornly refused to accept aid.

Then one Autumn day two small children called on her. They carried a large box of provisions.

"These were brought to the Harvest Festival," they told her. "They're for you."

Mrs Williams was about to refuse when she noticed the happy eagerness in the children's eyes. How could she thwart their efforts to think of others? She took the box with a smile, and, strangely, felt much easier in her mind as she put the goods away in her bare cupboard.

Of course it is better to give than to receive, but Mrs Williams learned that day that to accept help graciously is also a virtue.

SUNDAY—OCTOBER 18.

THOU shalt love thy neighbour as thyself.

MONDAY—OCTOBER 19.

HAVE you heard the message of the garden shears? It was passed on to me by an old man I once met in Sussex. He put it this way, " To achieve happiness, married couples should resemble a pair of garden shears—joined together so that they cannot be separated, often moving in opposite directions, yet punishing anyone coming between them."

TUESDAY—OCTOBER 20.

ONE mild misty morning in October I walked along a lane in Somerset. Suddenly the mist cleared and there in front of me in the haze sunshine were masses of lovely purple-pink foxgloves. I picked some of these " long purples " to press and remind me of this treasured moment.

Some time later I paid a visit to Edgbaston Parish Church, Birmingham, and noticed a memorial. It caught my eye because on it was a beautifully fashioned foxglove. It was the memorial to William Witheringham, the doctor who discovered that the foxglove could give digitalis, the well-known heart sedative. A lady at my side told me that she had some of these little brown pills in her handbag and that they had saved her life.

I looked again at the memorial in silence and remembered that lane in Somerset with it's purple-pink flowers—flowers that I know now are not only beautiful but useful and a blessing to mankind.

WEDNESDAY—OCTOBER 21.

THE Sunday school children had been very busy distributing flowers, fruit and vegetables from the harvest festival. They visited all the old folk in the district, especially those living alone, and presented them with little gifts, accompanied by a card from their church.

One old lady told me about it. " What a lovely surprise it was," she said, " when I opened the door and saw this sweet little girl holding a basket of fruit." She said it reminded her of her own Sunday school days, and she was so glad that the traditional harvest festival was still very much alive.

And she finished, " The fruit is quite delicious—but, you know, the thing I appreciated most of all was the fact that somebody had remembered me and sent to my door such a nice young person. It was like a breath of fresh air!"

THURSDAY—OCTOBER 22.

DO you like me, Mr Gay?" said my little friend Philippa.

" Of course, " I assured her.

" And will you ever forget me?"

" Forget you?" I answered. " A nice girl like you? No, I'll never forget you."

" That's good." Philippa seemed quite pleased. Then she started one of her innumerable little games.

" Knock, Knock," she said.

" Who's there?" I answered, always ready to join in.

" Philippa," she laughed. " You see—you've forgotten already!"

I always fall for it, don't I?

SUMMERTIME

Give me tranquil summer days
Beside a gentle stream,
Where cottage windows open wide
To catch the sun's bright gleam.

Lovely to stop and dream awhile,
To stand a bit and gaze,
And watch the speckled trout go by
And, like them, bask and laze!

FRIDAY—OCTOBER 23.

THE leader of the prayer meeting was a little concerned because, instead of the continuous chain of prayers from members of the group which he desired there were often long pauses.

In some impatience he said, " Keep the ball rolling, brothers and sisters, keep the ball rolling! Remember, the Devil takes advantage of every period of silence!"

Well, perhaps, but would it not have been wise for him to recognise that God can take advantage of every period of silence, too! " Be still, and know that I am God." He can speak to us in the silence and sometimes we tend to talk too much, even in prayer. A Chinese proverb reminds us, " God gave us only one mouth but two ears—therefore we ought to talk less and listen more."

SATURDAY—OCTOBER 24.

THIS world is an amazing place and we should all look around us in wonder from time to time.

I was impressed recently by some lines by an American poet, Dr William H. Carruth. There is not room here to give the full poem, but this is the remarkable first verse of " Autumn Deity":

A fire mist and a planet,
A crystal and a cell,
A jellyfish and a saurian,
And caves where the cave men dwell;
Then a sense of law and beauty,
And a face turned from the clod—
Some call it evolution,
But others call it God.

SUNDAY—OCTOBER 25.

GOD is faithful, who will not suffer you to be tempted above that ye are able.

MONDAY—OCTOBER 26.

THE first Henry Ford used to say that the Model A Ford would have been on the road six months earlier than it was if only he had insisted that his engineers had not worked on Sundays. So anxious were they to complete the project that they worked seven days a week. What they did not realise was that, in denying themselves the leisure of a rest day, they were in fact working less efficiently and slowing down the eventual completion of the task.

In Papua they have an interesting saying in support of the observance of Sunday: " We need a day for our souls to catch up with our bodies." So do we all.

TUESDAY—OCTOBER 27.

HAVE you had a disappointment?
Been feeling extra sad?
Does it seem as if the good things
Have a way of turning bad?

Then take some consolation
In the message written here;
For after troubled patches
Comes a time of special cheer.

The scales are always moving,
Sometimes up and sometimes down.
This morning's smiles will cancel out
Yesterday's dark frown.

WEDNESDAY—OCTOBER 28.

RICHARD ST. BARBE BAKER devoted his life to trees. In October 1979 he celebrated his 90th birthday. A few days earlier I heard him speak for a full hour, fluently and without any notes, on his career in forestry and his long fight to save the great redwood trees of California.

It was a fascinating talk. But what impressed me most was his testimony that he enjoyed every new day that God gave him better than the day before; and in the introduction to one of his books he concludes with a similar thought: "To me each day is more wonderful than the previous one and my wish for the reader is that he or she may enjoy that same experience."

A delightful thought from an exhilarating nonagenarian.

THURSDAY—OCTOBER 29.

I HAVE just been re-reading *Larkrise to Candleford*, Flora Thompson's delightful book about Oxfordshire village life last century. Although remote from the capital, the little community became enthused with the Jubilee of Queen Victoria, and many were the stories which circulated about the Queen.

One concerned an occasion when some church workers were invited to tea in the drawing-room at Osborne. One poor lady, unaccustomed to taking tea with Royalty, dropped a slice of cake on the floor. One of the ladies-in-waiting was tactless enough to smile at her discomfiture, whereupon the Queen, noticing what had happened, called for a slice of cake, dropped it on the floor and bade the lady who had smiled sweep up both pieces!

FRIDAY—OCTOBER 30.

I LOVE the story of the boy who came to the harvest festival with his friends, bringing five apples. The minister, who knew that all these little thank-offerings had been provided by the families, announced to the children that he would personally thank their parents. The lad with the five apples piped up, rather shame-facedly, "When you thank my mum, please remember to thank her for *six* apples!"

SATURDAY—OCTOBER 31.

HAVE you ever heard of the hymn that was written on the back of a playing card? It's one we all know well—"Rock Of Ages." The story is that Augustus Toplady was caught in a thunderstorm in the Mendip Hills. He looked around for shelter but there seemed to be none within reach. Then he spied a cleft in the rocks, its entrance so narrow he could hardly squeeze in.

As he crouched in the shelter, listening to the storm raging outside, he was inspired to write the verses which were to become famous throughout the world.

Rock of Ages, cleft for me
Let me hide myself in Thee.

As the words flowed through his mind he looked around for something on which to write them down before he forgot them. But among the rocks he could see nothing he could use except an old playing card which someone had cast aside. He picked it up and in the gloom wrote them down. The card as well as the hymn became famous throughout the world and landed in America where it is a valued treasure.

NOVEMBER

SUNDAY—NOVEMBER 1.

CHARITY suffereth long, and is kind.

MONDAY—NOVEMBER 2.

HAND on heart is a phrase that seems to have gone out of fashion.

It once was reasonably common, conveying that the speaker believed he was telling the absolute truth or would faithfully carry out a promise.

I've never known where the phrase comes from. I always took it to be simply that the speaker was putting his hand on his heart as a token of his truthfulness. Now I'm beginning to wonder, after talking to a friend back from a business trip round the Middle East.

At a Customs Post he was one of a queue, being taken one at a time into the official's shed. When my friend was called, the Customs officer asked him a few commonplace questions, standing face to face and watching him carefully. Then he stretched forward and gently placed his hand on my friend's shirt, just over his heart. Studying him intently, he asked if my friend was carrying any drugs.

Afterwards he smilingly explained to my friend that no matter how experienced a smuggler he was up against, somehow the hand on the heart questioning always produced a response that made him instantly suspicious of a guilty person.

Hand on heart? Yes, it is a promise not to be used lightly.

TUESDAY—NOVEMBER 3.

YEARS ago I used to visit an old lady who was completely blind but who, in spite of her handicap, was one of the most lively and cheerful companions imaginable.

Commenting once on her blindness she used a sentence which has stayed in my mind over the years. I never knew whether it was original or whether she had heard it somewhere but it was certainly the secret of her own indomitable spirit. "I am glad," she said, "that the Lord saw fit to make me blind and not deaf, for blindness only cuts you off from things; deafness cuts you off from people."

I think most of us would be hard put to it if we had to make the choice, but what an amazing tribute that is to the importance of counting our blessings and not our burdens.

WEDNESDAY—NOVEMBER 4.

RICHARD BYRD, the Antarctic explorer, wrote, "It was on my lonely vigil during the long Polar night that I learned the power of silence. The values and problems of life sorted themselves out when I began to listen."

Those intrepid travellers, Mildred Cable and Francesca French, found the same thing in the Gobi Desert: "The solitudes provoked reflection; the wide spaces gave a right sense of proportion; the silences forbade triviality."

Fortunately, we do not need to go as far as the Antarctic or the Gobi Desert for this experience. The quietness of the countryside, of a church building, of a garden, even of our own room can provide for us the healing power of silence.

THURSDAY—NOVEMBER 5.

WE'D been at Dave and Marie's wedding, so we were delighted to receive a card from them while on their honeymoon. The message was short. It just said, "We are at Loggerheads with each other."

This caused not a little consternation—until we noticed the name of the beauty spot where they were staying. It was Loggerheads in North Staffordshire!

FRIDAY—NOVEMBER 6.

THERE was once a boy called Richard who lived with his parents in a cottage on the side of a grassy hill. Down below was a valley with a little river running through, and opposite rose tall, rocky hills with sheep grazing on the springy grass. One day Richard wanted to do something very badly, but his parents would not agree. He begged and begged, but they wouldn't give in, and, finally he rushed out of the house, very angry, shouting at the top of his voice, "I hate you! I hate you!"

Then, across from the other side of the valley, came a little voice, "I hate you. I hate you." He stopped, amazed, wondering who on earth could be over there saying they hated him, when he hadn't done anything to them. He was so curious, he forgot he was cross and ran back inside and told his father about it.

His father smiled and said, "Come with me." Together, they went outside, and his father called loudly, "I love you. I love you." And back came the voice, "I love you. I love you." His father took Richard's hand. "That's an echo. It's a reminder to us that we get back what we give."

SATURDAY—NOVEMBER 7.

I REMEMBER childhood dreams,
The memories still stay,
When all the world was full of joy
And life was full of play.
And though the adult world is hard,
I still keep in my heart
A glimpse of that same wonder
I captured at the start.

SUNDAY—NOVEMBER 8.

A MERRY heart maketh a cheerful countenance.

MONDAY—NOVEMBER 9.

I HAVE just been reading these words by James C. Penney, an American who was born in 1875 and died in his 97th year:

" I am grateful for all my problems. As each of them was overcome I became stronger and more able to meet those yet to come. I grew on all my difficulties."

Those words, written towards the end of a long and eventful life, remind me of an old lady I knew when I was a boy. One day I ran into her kitchen and saw her slicing lemons. I helped myself to a slice and she smiled at the face I pulled while sucking it. I watched her put the rest of the slices into a large earthenware jug, add sugar and honey, and then pour on boiling water.

" I'll tell you something, Francis," she said. " It's a great day when we learn to turn life's lemons into lemonade."

Thinking about it now, wasn't she saying the same thing as James C. Penney? It was just that she had a more homely way of saying it!

TUESDAY—NOVEMBER 10.

ROSEMARY GLUBB wrote these charming lines which she calls simply " Thank You."

Thank You, God, for a quiet night,
Thank You for my morning tea,
For the dawn breaking, grey or light,
And for the tasks which wait for me.

Thank You for all the homely things—
My small dog greeting me bright-eyed,
My cat whose purr a welcome sings,
Warm food Your bounty does provide.

Help me this day just to be good,
To pray, and praise You all the while.
Whatever be my changing mood,
Lord, let me not forget to smile.

WEDNESDAY—NOVEMBER 11.

THIS year several million poppies will be sold, every one of them made by 120 disabled ex-servicemen at the Royal British Legion poppy factory at Richmond, Surrey.

The custom of wearing poppies was conceived by a Frenchwoman called Madame Guerin in 1921. She had been influenced by some lines of the Scottish-Canadian poet, John McCrae, written while he was serving as an army medical officer in 1915:

If ye break faith with us who die
We shall not sleep, though poppies grow
In Flanders fields.

So I take my poppy very seriously. By wearing it I feel that I am not only helping the disabled. I am also keeping faith with those who lost their lives in two terrible world wars.

THURSDAY—NOVEMBER 12.

ONE of Charles Dickens's lesser-known stories is *The Haunted Man* which tells of a chemist whose life was plagued with unhappy memories. At last a spirit came to him promising to remove his distress in exchange for the man's power of memory.

The man agreed eagerly, but when he found that he had no recollection of the good as well as of the bad, he realised his life was impoverished, not enriched. He begged for the restoration of his power of memory, and the story ends with the prayer, "Lord keep my memory green."

Of course we all have memories we would gladly rub out, but there are so many other things, aren't there, that we would love to recall even more vividly than we do. Yes, a "green memory" is a blessing indeed.

FRIDAY—NOVEMBER 13.

I ONCE read of a man who had a dream that he was walking on sand. His footsteps were clearly defined but at some point another set of footprints ran alongside his own. He could not help noticing that it was where the going was easiest that the mystery footprints appeared.

He knew instinctively that the invisible companion was the Lord and, remembering the course of his own life, he could not help calling out, "You promised to walk with me all the way if I followed You. Why was it that when it was hardest I had to walk alone and when it was easiest, You walked with me?"

And in the dream, the Lord replied, "The double steps were where I walked with you, but the single steps were where I *carried* you."

SATURDAY—NOVEMBER 14.

THE people of Coventry will always remember the night of November 14, 1940, when their city suffered the longest air raid of the War. Next day those who were brave enough walked through the ruins of their beloved city to the remains of its cathedral. There they looked towards the sky with bitter and vengeful eyes.

But eventually a miracle happened. Instead of revenge there came forgiveness. Taking two charred beams which had been part of the cathedral roof, they tied them together in the form of a cross and set it up where the cathedral altar had once stood.

Today the cross is surrounded by a beautiful new cathedral. And in a prominent place are these words: " Father, forgive."

It's wonderful that Coventry Cathedral rose again in such splendour and beauty. It's even more wonderful that it was rebuilt in a spirit of love, charity and forgiveness. That is the real miracle of Coventry.

SUNDAY—NOVEMBER 15.

FOR as the heavens are higher than the earth, so are my ways higher than your ways, and my thoughts than your thoughts.

MONDAY—NOVEMBER 16.

OF course, you have a good excuse
For grumbling night and day.
This old world is a sorry place—
You tread a lonely way.
But moans don't make life's fog less thick;
It's sunny smiles that do the trick.

TUESDAY—NOVEMBER 17.

YOU meet some interesting people on the train.

The worried middle-aged man next to me had been visiting his mother. "It's a problem," he told me. "She's very old and she no longer recognises any of the family. We often catch her with a faraway look in her eyes."

The lady across from us spoke up at this point and told us she was matron of an old people's home.

"Don't pity your mother," she said to the man. "She's probably years back in the past, at a dance or playing with her family when you were babies. Last week, one of my old ladies told me quite happily that she was going to visit her mother, to have hot, toasted muffins and cocoa.

"You see, old age robs people of a great deal, but it leaves the precious gift of memory. They can't remember what they had for lunch, but can recall every detail of something that happened 70 years ago. Your mother doesn't have any more stress and strain in her life—she's been through all that. Now she is just enjoying reliving the past."

Roses in December . . .

WEDNESDAY—NOVEMBER 18.

NOT what you get, but what you give,
Not what you say, but how you live,
Giving the world the love it needs,
Living the life of noble deeds.

Not whence you came, but whither bound,
Not what you have, but whether found,
Strong in the right, the good, the true,
These are the things worthwhile to you.

REAL SKILL

It's not so easy as it looks
At thatching to excel;
Time and care—you need 'em both
To roof a cottage well.

THURSDAY—NOVEMBER 19.

JOHN WESLEY, the great 18th century evangelist, had a very ready wit.

One day he was walking down a particularly narrow alleyway when he was confronted by a pompous man who shouted, " Step aside, fellow! I never make way for fools."

" Oh," replied John Wesley, smartly stepping aside to let him pass, " *I* always do!"

FRIDAY—NOVEMBER 20.

LAST week I regretfully said good-bye to a dear old friend—an elderly, rather threadbare, tweed suit.

I remember the day, many years ago, when the two of us called into a gent's outfitters and I said I'd like to see some tweeds. The assistant looked me up and down for a moment, then pounced upon a greenish two-piece and had the jacket on me in a jiffy.

It fitted like a glove. Sensible shade, too. I glanced at the Lady of the House. " Yes, I like it," she pronounced. " Fine, I'll take it," I told the assistant.

But my better half had strolled to another rail of tweeds. She wondered aloud if a brownish shade wouldn't perhaps be a change. There was also one in interesting tones of blue and after that she wondered if . . .

I tried them all, but in the end chose the greenish one I'd originally picked. The Lady of the House was very pleased. " You know, Francis," she said as we left the shop. " You can't tell which suit's best until you've tried on some you don't like!"

A woman's philosophy is truly wonderful!

SATURDAY—NOVEMBER 21.

THE elm tree was showing definite signs of disease so the authorities ordered it to be cut down. But one of the woodmen, Jim Scott, spotted something amongst the branches. He climbed up and discovered a bird's nest with three eggs in it.

"We can't cut the tree down yet," Jim declared, and his colleagues agreed. After a bit of debate, the authorities agreed to allow the tree to stand until the eggs were hatched and the young birds away from the nest.

Two months later, the tree was felled. Jim Scott was fascinated by the ingenious way the nest had been made. Bit by bit he pulled the twigs, grass and moss apart, and discovered the bird had also used hundreds of tiny scraps of paper, tightly rolled. When he looked more closely, he saw some of the scraps were from a Bible.

And on one were the words from the 84th psalm, "Yea, the sparrow hath found an house."

SUNDAY—NOVEMBER 22.

PEACE be within thy walls, and prosperity within thy palaces.

MONDAY—NOVEMBER 23.

A FATHER came home from work to find his little son busily drawing with a crayon. "What picture are you drawing?" he asked.

"God," said the boy. The father smiled. "You can't draw God," he said. "No one knows what he looks like."

"They will soon," said his son, bending to his task.

TUESDAY—NOVEMBER 24.

I WAS walking through a cemetery recently, and, you know, I found it a surprisingly cheerful place. The sun was shining, the birds singing, and beautiful flowers were everywhere. What is more, in this peaceful setting I saw carved on the gravestones so much evidence of love and affection—such as this tribute that a husband had given to his late wife:

" Without you no perfect day."

I thought it was one of the loveliest epitaphs I had ever seen. Although so short and simple, it speaks volumes about a happy marriage.

WEDNESDAY—NOVEMBER 25.

I CANNOT claim to be much of a climber but I did once allow a couple of friends to lure me on to some rocky crags. I confess that by the time we were half way up, the little enthusiasm I'd had was gone and life had become a battle against treacherous footholds, loose stones and jagged boulders.

The struggle upwards seemed a hazardous waste of energy—until at last we reached the top. Words would fail me if I tried to describe the beauty that opened out before my wondering eyes, the range upon range of cloud-kissed peaks spreading as far as my friends and I could see. How white the fluffy clouds were, and how majestically they sailed across the heavenly blue!

That climb taught me not to fret about the vexations of an hour or the weariness of life's problems. Whenever the going is hard I remind myself that a summit of achievement lies ahead and I will reach it if I press on and overcome the hardships on the way.

THURSDAY—NOVEMBER 26.

I HAVE just been reading John Braine's book about his fellow-writer and fellow-Yorkshireman, J. B. Priestley. He writes about Priestley's cheerfulness and optimism, and likens him to a character in one of Ernest Hemingway's books, Colonel Cantwell, who "never felt sad in the morning. Even if nothing went right yesterday he hopes that something wonderful will happen today . . . he is sustained always by that moment of joy in the morning."

How much better for us to begin the day like that, rather than that people should say of us, "He got out of bed on the wrong side this morning!"

FRIDAY—NOVEMBER 27.

ISN'T it odd how early in life we get the idea we are right and others wrong?

I've just heard of the time young Brian, nearly four, went with his grandad to an agricultural show. They passed the brightly-painted tractors and combine harvesters and other marvels and wandered around inspecting cattle and sheep with a critical eye, for Brian is a farmer's son. Here and there they went until—panic!—Brian went missing.

Grandad searched high and low, but the lad was nowhere to be found. Then word came over a loudspeaker that a small boy was waiting to be collected at the reception tent. When an agitated grandfather arrived, upset and breathless, there was Brian sitting on a table, sucking lemonade through a straw and swinging his legs happily.

"Grandad," he reproved. "Why didn't you stay with me instead of getting lost?"

SATURDAY—NOVEMBER 28.

A WORKMAN was talking to his new apprentice and trying to find out a little about his background and interests, but he was not getting very far. To his question, "What do you do with your spare time, for instance?" he received only the vaguest of replies, but he plugged away at it. "Do you read any books?" he asked.

"Well," replied the boy doubtfully, "I used to read a bit—before I grew up."

There are things we ought to grow out of, but I fear sometimes we grow out of the wrong things. It was a great scholar on whose tombstone were inscribed the words: "He died learning." It's a true saying that we are never too old to learn.

SUNDAY—NOVEMBER 29.

BLESSED is he that considereth the poor: the Lord will deliver him in time of trouble.

MONDAY—NOVEMBER 30.

THE beginners' dancing class was giving a display.

For the final item, the children had to perform something of their own choosing. The first little girl gave her impression of a butterfly. The next interpreted a swan, another a deer, and so on. Last was five-year-old Irene. She baffled everyone by wobbling from side to side and finally disappearing into the wings with a big lurch.

Stumped, the dancing teacher asked what she was supposed to represent. Irene gave a triumphant, gappy smile and answered—"A loose tooth!"

DECEMBER

TUESDAY—DECEMBER 1.

HERE'S a story with a smile in it. Dionysius, the tyrant of Syracuse in ancient Sicily, wrote very bad verse which no one dared to criticise until one day the poet Philoxenus told his ruler the truth. Philoxenus was promptly sent to the galleys for his pains.

Some time later, Dionysius summoned him and read some new verses he had written, confident that the poet would have learned his lesson. Philoxenus listened a while and then got up. Much surprised, Dionysius asked him where he was going. " Back to the galleys!" was the answer.

WEDNESDAY—DECEMBER 2.

WHENEVER Queen Victoria stayed at Balmoral, various ministers came to the castle to conduct the Sunday services. The Queen showed her appreciation by giving each of them an autographed picture of herself.

George Matheson, the blind minister who wrote the much loved hymn " O Love that wilt not let me go," was one of the preachers who went to the castle, but what could the Queen give to him? A picture would be useless. Instead she placed in his hands a small bust of herself. His sensitive fingers would be able to feel the features of the Sovereign he was unable to see.

Few of us are sufficiently distinguished to give away busts of ourselves, but we can all emulate the Queen's example by being thoughtful and considerate—especially to any handicapped people we meet along the way.

THURSDAY—DECEMBER 3.

I KNOW many of you like the ten-second sermons which come my way. Here's the latest selection—

The harder you fall, the higher you bounce.

Worry is like sand in an oyster. A little produces a pearl; too much kills the oyster.

Don't be so busy learning the tricks that you never learn the trade.

A lie travels all round the world while truth is putting on her boots.

All sunshine and nothing else makes a desert.

Noah managed to build the ark because he had no committee to help him.

If you want to be rich, try spending yourself.

FRIDAY—DECEMBER 4.

I WAS standing in the High Street, chatting with Willie Graham. Willie is a Sunday School teacher and the youngsters love him.

Suddenly across the street raced seven-year-old Peter Brown, a boy in Willie's class.

"Excuse me, Mr Graham," said Peter breathlessly. "It's your birthday, isn't it? Many happy returns!"

Willie beamed. "It's very clever of you to remember, Peter." He fumbled in his pocket. "I think you deserve a sweet," he said.

Just as Peter was saying, "Thank you" and dashing off, all in one movement, Willie stopped him.

"By the way, how did you remember it was my birthday, Peter?" he asked.

"Oh, I couldn't forget," said the little boy, very seriously. "It's the same day as the birthday of my dog, Ruffie."

SATURDAY—DECEMBER 5.

THE slightest word of comfort
To help us on our way,
The slightest smile from someone
To brighten up our day;
The slightest act of kindness
To lessen care and such—
All these cost so little,
But they mean so very much.

SUNDAY—DECEMBER 6.

FOR the earth is the Lord's, and the fulness thereof.

MONDAY—DECEMBER 7.

ONE birthday when I was a boy I received both a Meccano and a carpentry set. With the Meccano I planned to make a windmill, complete with sails that turned. As for the saw, hammers and nails of the carpentry set—well, there were no limits to my ambitious projects.

The limits came when I actually got down to assembling the windmill and trying to make a small canoe. Both were failures.

"Oh, what's the use of trying!" I remember exclaiming, as my grandfather and I examined the canoe that had overturned in his water butt.

"Never say that!" Grandpa declared. "There's *every* use in trying!"

He encouraged me to have another go, and while I chiselled out a fresh piece of wood he shared one of his secrets with me. I have treasured it ever since: "Remember, lad," he said, "ideals are like the stars. We may never reach them but they are the best guides we have."

TUESDAY—DECEMBER 8.

MRS Georgina Hall, like many of us, loves walking on crisp new snow, and has sent me this poem which she calls " Winter Walk ":

I walked through endless fields of white,
A wonderland of snow,
Mist-shrouded hilltops high above,
A frozen path below.
Imprinted footsteps followed me
Like ghosts that walked behind,
A thousand dreams and fantasies
Re-echoed in my mind.

The lanes transformed were blossoming
In snowflakes starkly white,
The skies shone blue above my head,
A dream of pure delight,
A phantom dream in phantom world
But joy still ruled the day.
Forgetting cold and heart's dismay
I sang upon my way.

WEDNESDAY—DECEMBER 9.

IT takes a lot of work to make a Christmas cake. Not just in the kitchen, but all over the world. For just consider the ingredients: butter from New Zealand, currants from Greece, wheat from Canada, cherries and angelica from France, sugar from the West Indies, oranges from Israel, sultanas from Australia, spices from Ceylon, lemons from Spain, and so on.

When you think of it, the whole world is working together to make your Christmas cake. Perhaps one day the world will work together in the same spirit to produce the true and lasting peace that is the message and hope of Christmas.

MIX WELL . . .

It's fun helping Mummy and learning to bake,
'Specially when it's your own birthday cake.

THURSDAY—DECEMBER 10.

WHAT a wonderful day it was when Mrs Climie of Meigle, Perthshire, celebrated her 100th birthday! On the November day when she received her telegram of congratulations from the Queen, she kept " open house " to the constant stream of visitors who came to her door.

The amazing thing was that all the people who had come to offer her their best wishes came away feeling that *she* had done something for *them.* And she had. For are there greater gifts than a ready smile and a cheerful spirit?

It does us all good to know someone like Mrs Climie.

FRIDAY—DECEMBER 11.

DR LLOYD DOUGLAS, author of the famous novels *The Robe* and *The Big Fisherman,* tells us of visiting a friend, a somewhat eccentric violin teacher.

" Well, and what's the good news today?" Dr Douglas greeted him. For answer the teacher stepped over to a metal device suspended from a silk thread and struck it a sharp blow with a little mallet: " That's the good news for today! That note, my friend, is ' A '. It was ' A ' yesterday. It will be ' A ' tomorrow, next week, in a thousand years. The soprano next door wobbles abominably, the tenor over yonder sings unspeakably flat, and the piano across the hall is out of tune. Noise and confusion all about me, but *that* is ' A '."

In a world of chance and change we can find comfort in the fact that there are some things that never change—truth, beauty, goodness and love among them. We should hold them fast.

SATURDAY—DECEMBER 12.

THERE'S always something to smile at in the letters that come from Mildred Murdoch, of Riverside, California.

But always that something is well worth remembering. In her last letter, for instance, I was struck by these words:

When you come to the end of your tether, tie a knot and hang on!

SUNDAY—DECEMBER 13.

THE eternal God is thy refuge, and underneath are the everlasting arms.

MONDAY—DECEMBER 14.

WE had a visitor recently—Father Joseph.

He's an old missionary friend I've known since I was a boy. He'd just returned after a few years' work around the globe and for hours on end we were entertained by anecdotes from Gambia, Guatemala and India. My favourite, though, was his introduction to Chinese writing.

He took a felt pen and drew on a sheet of paper an intricate design. "This is the Chinese way of depicting a house," he explained. He drew another design, not unlike a pear-shaped figure eight. "And this," he said, "is the Chinese character for 'woman.'"

Then our friend drew the woman as if she was in the house. This was the symbol for peace, he told us.

He drew on and, this time, he put two of the women characters inside the house. "And that, believe it or not," he said, "is the Chinese symbol for war!"

TUESDAY—DECEMBER 15.

WHEN sorrow falls upon our day
And dark and lonely is the way,
How strange, we often find relief
In lightening someone else's grief.

WEDNESDAY—DECEMBER 16.

A SMALL boy once asked his mother a profound theological question: " Mum," he said, " why is it that God puts vitamins in spinach and cod liver oil and not in lemonade and chewing gum?"

Profound indeed! So often, it seems the things we like are not good for us, and the things which are good for us, we do not like. But God in his wisdom has made it so and we should be poorer, not richer, if we did not sometimes have to discipline ourselves to do the things we really do not want to do, and to deny ourselves sometimes the things which seem pleasant and desirable. That way lies the development of character—and it goes deeper than vitamins!

THURSDAY—DECEMBER 17.

YOU don't often read notice-boards that are sheer poetry, but I don't know how else to describe this one that was seen on a young tree in a Spanish park: " I am a tree. You who would raise your hand against me, remember that I am the heat of your hearth on cold nights; the friendly shade screening you from summer heat; the beam of your house; the board of your table; the bed on which you lie; the timber of your boat; the handle of your hoe; the wood of your cradle; the shell of your coffin. Harm me not."

FRIDAY—DECEMBER 18.

RALPH WALDO EMERSON, the great 19th century American writer and poet, once gave this advice:

"Finish every day and be done with it. You have done what you could. Some blunders and absurdities may have crept in: forget them as soon as you can. Tomorrow is a new day: begin it well and serenely and with too high a spirit to be worried over your old nonsense. This day is all that is good and fair. It is too dear, with its hopes and invitations, to waste a moment on the yesterdays."

SATURDAY—DECEMBER 19.

WHEN the evenings were drawing in, the Lady of the House spent much of her time dressmaking.

Her way of going about it intrigued me. She spent ages laying out patterns on the dining-room table, fitting them this way and that, measuring carefully until she was satisfied all was as it should be. Then and only then did she take up her scissors and cut out the material, ready for the sewing machine.

When I complimented her on the care with which she went about it, she smiled. "You gave me the clue yourself, years ago," she said.

"Me?" I echoed incredulously, for I know nothing about dressmaking, needless to say.

"When you were building those bookshelves," she smiled. "You said something I've never forgotten—'Measure twice, cut once!'"

And, though I say it myself, it's as good a maxim for living as for wood or velvet!

GOING HOME

After the pleasure
And thrills of play,
How sweet the peace
At close of day!

SUNDAY—DECEMBER 20.

GLORY to God in the highest, and on earth peace, good will toward men.

MONDAY—DECEMBER 21.

HIS name is long since forgotten, but he was a wise man who, long ago, declared, "Success simply consists in getting up once oftener than you fall down."

TUESDAY—DECEMBER 22.

CHRISTMAS time is carol time. There are many lovely carols, and we all have our favourites. One of the most delightful begins

I saw three ships come sailing by
On Christmas Day in the morning.

It makes a pretty picture, and one to kindle the imagination, for there are three ships which have real significance for us at this season.

One is *wor-ship*, most definitely a Christmas ship. In writing of the first Christmas St Matthew mentioned it: "And when they were come into the house, they saw the young child with Mary his mother, and fell down and worshipped Him."

Another ship that comes sailing in at Christmas is *friend-ship*. For this is a time when we think of our friends and send greetings to those who live at a distance.

The third ship is *steward-ship*. A steward is one who is trusted to serve. Serving was something that He who came at Christmas was most emphatic about.

May these three ships come sailing into your hearts and homes this Christmas, bringing their precious gifts of joy and peace.

WEDNESDAY—DECEMBER 23.

GIVE freely of your time, my friend,
It's more precious far than money.
A kindly word, a helping hand,
Can change dark skies to sunny.

THURSDAY—DECEMBER 24.

MY grandfather exerted a powerful influence over me when I was a child. Even now — many years later — rarely a day goes by without my recalling some aspect of his wise and kindly philosophy.

One late winter's afternoon just before Christmas I had gone into the nearby town with my grandfather to do some shopping. Dusk was falling, it was raining and cold and the pavements were crowded. Suddenly, from behind us a hand slapped my grandfather's shoulder and a hearty voice bellowed in our ears, " Happy Christmas — how are you?" We turned and looked into the face of a complete stranger. The man looked confused and blushed with embarrassment as he said, " Oh — I am sorry . . . I mistook you for somebody else."

" Sorry?" echoed my grandfather. " Why should you be sorry? Things have come to a pretty pass if we feel that we have to apologise for wishing somebody a happy Christmas and asking how they are!"

He held out his hand and the man's face cleared as he shook it.

" Aye," he agreed, " you're right. Happy Christmas to you!"

Somehow, as we walked on, that street seemed to be a warmer, less impersonal and altogether a happier place. And as you see, I never forgot it.

FRIDAY—DECEMBER 25.

CHRISTMAS DAY would not be the same for millions without the traditional Christmas Message by Her Majesty the Queen. Of all her encouraging words over the years I particularly remember her message in 1975. It is a tonic for those who feel lost in the vastness of the world and that's probably all of us at some time or other.

The Queen said, " We are all different, but each of us has his own best to offer. The responsibility for the way we live life, with all its challenges, sadness and joy, is ours alone. If we do this well, it will be also good for our neighbours.

" If you throw a stone into a pool, the ripples go on spreading outwards. A big stone can cause waves, but even the smallest pebble changes the whole pattern of the water. Our daily actions are like those ripples: each one makes a difference, even the smallest."

SATURDAY—DECEMBER 26.

TASTES in reading differ as in everything else, but I personally like the books I read to have a happy ending. Perhaps this is why I find the late Arthur Gossip's description of the New Testament particularly inspiring. This one time Professor of Trinity College, Glasgow, described it as " the happiest thing in literature, with the sound of singing in it everywhere." He then pointed out that it opens with the choir of angels over Bethlehem on the first Christmas night, and closes with the Hallelujah Chorus of the redeemed.

That's quite a song cycle, isn't it?

CHRISTMAS WISH

If you're very, very careful
When you're dressing up the tree,
When Santa comes on Christmas Eve
How pleased he's going to be!

SUNDAY—DECEMBER 27.

A WORD spoken in due season, how good is it!

MONDAY—DECEMBER 28.

PABLO CASALS, the world famous cellist, published his biography when he was 93 and in it he had this to say about work:

" Work helps to prevent one getting old. I for one cannot dream of retiring. Not now, or ever. Retire? The word is alien to me. My work is my life. I cannot think of one without the other. The man who works and is never bored is never old. Work and interest in worthwhile things are the best remedy for age. Each day I am reborn. Each day I must begin again."

Not all of us have work which engrosses us in the way Casals found, but we can all develop " an interest in worthwhile things ".

TUESDAY—DECEMBER 29.

HAVE you ever noticed that the Bible does not give the exact number of wise men who came to visit the Baby Jesus? (In the original Greek the word was Magi). We know, of course, that they came bearing three costly gifts: gold, frankincense and myrrh. But there could easily have been only two men—or four men, or more.

Which leads me to share an old legend with you, that of the fourth wise man who turned back from the all-important journey because the going was hard. He began, side by side with his friends, heading for the new and shining star, but he gave up before he reached his goal.

As I say, it's only an old legend—but I think it holds a valuable lesson for us. Don't you agree?

WEDNESDAY—DECEMBER 30.

JOHNNY and his twin brother asked for an apple.

" They are so big," said their mother, " I think you had better share one between you."

She handed it to Ian, the other twin: " Now, share that with Johnny, and share it like a Christian."

Ian did not, as might have been expected, cut it carefully in half. Instead, he made one large piece, and one small. Then he turned to Johnny:

" Now, you choose—like a Christian!"

THURSDAY—DECEMBER 31.

MANY a family gathers round the piano for a New Year sing-song, and there's one " must " for an occasion like that—" Bless This House."

It was written by Helen Taylor who was brought up in a lonely farmhouse amid quiet Essex countryside. To find a job she had to go to London. She lived in a dark, damp basement flat and it was there that her mind travelled back to relive the happy days of her childhood.

She wrote well-loved songs like " Come To the Fair " and " I Passed By Your Window." Then one she called " Bless The House." There was something about the song she wasn't happy with. She couldn't put her finger on it so she took it to the famous tenor John McCormack for his views. He liked the melody and the words, but he had reservations about the title. Wouldn't " Bless *This* House " be better?

That was it! Helen agreed, and the song went on to win a place in the hearts of those who treasure all that the love of home stands for.

Where the Photographs were taken

MIRACLE — *Nr. Newtonmore, Inverness-shire.*
LISTENING — *Pistyll Cain Falls, Merioneth.*
THE GIFT — *Beverley Market, Yorkshire.*
THE GOOD WAY — *Cleveland Hills, Yorkshire.*
THE DEEP — *Berryl's Point, Newquay, Cornwall.*
THE DISTANT VIEW — *Talyllyn, Merioneth.*
FREEDOM — *Balnacoil Falls, River Blackwater, Sutherland.*
BEAUTY — *Naunton, Gloucestershire.*
DREAMING — *Mellerstain, Berwickshire.*
PARTNERS — *Bridgnorth, Shropshire.*
THE CROSSING — *River Dove, Derbyshire.*
QUIET HAUNTS — *Clovelly, Devon.*
PLEASURE — *Culzean Castle, Ayrshire.*
SANCTUARY — *Glen Etive, Argyll.*
GOOD SERVANT — *Castle Lane, Warwick.*
FOR ALL AGES — *Ravenglass Railway, Cumberland.*
PATIENCE — *Topiary, Levens Hall, Westmorland.*
DAY OUT — *Castle Loch, Lochmaben, Dumfriesshire.*
SUMMERTIME — *Allerford, Somerset.*
GOING HOME — *North Berwick, East Lothian.*

Printed and Published by D. C. THOMSON & Co., LTD.,
185 Fleet Street, London EC4A 2HS.
© D. C. Thomson & Co., Ltd., 1980.
ISBN 0 85116 197 9

PERTH AND KINROSS DISTRICT LIBRARIES

This book is due for return on or before the last date indicated on label. Renewals may be obtained on application.

First edition

Published by Ladybird Books Ltd Loughborough Leicestershire UK
Ladybird Books Inc Auburn Maine 04210 USA

© LADYBIRD BOOKS LTD MCMXC
All rights reserved. No part of this publication may be reproduced, stored in a retrieval system, or transmitted in any form or by any means, electronic, mechanical, photo-copying, recording or otherwise, without the prior consent of the copyright owner.

Printed in England